Holy Grounds

HOLY GROUNDS

The Surprising
Connection
between
Coffee and Faith—
From Dancing
Goats to
Satan's Drink

Tim Schenck

Fortress Press

Minneapolis

Photo Credits
Author Photo: Ben Schenck
Pages 13, 37, 165, and 190: Bram de Hoogh

Cover design: Brad Norr

Print ISBN: 978-1-5064-4823-7
eBook ISBN: 978-1-5064-4824-4

The paper used in this publication meets the minimum requirements of American
National Standard for Information Sciences—Permanence of Paper for Printed
Library Materials, ANSI Z329.48-1984.

Manufactured in the U.S.A.

In memory of John Sherrill (1923–2017)
author, parishioner, coffee drinker, friend

CONTENTS

Coffee Connections

Black as the devil, hot as hell, pure as an angel, sweet as love.
That's the recipe for coffee.

—Charles Maurice de Talleyrand,
nineteenth-century French diplomat

When it comes to coffee, I'm a late adopter. While my college fraternity brothers tossed back herculean quantities during late-night study sessions, I didn't touch the stuff. As an army officer, while members of my platoon sucked down coffee with reckless abandon, I remained an outlier. When I managed political campaigns

1

and coffee was the jet fuel of marathon strategy sessions, I passed. At post-church coffee hour, while everyone drank coffee and critiqued the pastor's sermon, I drank lemonade.

Miraculously, I also endured a coffee-drinking wife, seminary, and one child without drinking coffee. The combination of two children under the age of two and full-time work in parish ministry, however, put me over the edge. And once I slipped down the rabbit hole of coffee consumption, a journey of discovery emerged that continues to unfold.

Coffee Narratives

Coffee often evokes the power of connection through personal narrative. Ask anyone when they first discovered the joys of coffee and prepare to be regaled with glimpses into their life story. Coffee can serve as an entry point into interpersonal relationships and shed light upon a person's values and most deeply held beliefs. In answering the simple question "When did you become a coffee drinker?" a person shares much of their life journey.

My parents began every day with freshly brewed coffee. In fact, their actions foreshadowed the Starbucks-driven coffee craze, as they ground whole-bean coffee purchased from specialty shops while most of America still scooped it out of giant tin cans. The sound of the grinder and the irresistible aroma of coffee in my own kitchen always remind me of the comforts and simplicities of childhood.

My late father, a symphony orchestra conductor, had a special relationship with the owner of the local coffee shop in Baltimore's Hampden neighborhood. I often accompanied him on his excursions to what was then a rather seedy side of town and is now one of Baltimore's hippest areas, chock full of trendy restaurants and coffeehouses.

At The Coffee Mill, a dazzling variety of whole-bean coffees sat in plastic bins with big scoops while the aroma overwhelmed the senses. Customers shoveled beans into bags, then brought them to the counter for weighing. The regulars, mostly men, were a mix of Baltimore's intelligentsia, artists, and urban pioneers. It wasn't a café—you couldn't actually *buy* a cup of coffee—but no one seemed hurried as they browsed the bins and chatted with fellow patrons.

One year, the owner, seeking a catchy, evocative name for a new blend, gave some beans to my dad to sample, asking him to help christen the roast. Which, I recall with great pride, he did. For many years after we moved from Baltimore to New York, you could still show up at The Coffee Mill and pick up a bag of Allegro con Brio.

Allegro, an Italian word, indicates a brisk or lively tempo in musical scores. *Con brio* is another musical direction meaning *with vigor*. So I can only imagine the newly christened coffee was bright, lively, and strong. Too bad I never got to taste it before The Coffee Mill closed down, after nearly three decades, in 2003.

I'm not sure why my parents never offered me a taste of their beloved coffee. I mean, they were pretty liberal about letting me and my brother try new things. My mother, a gourmet cook who authored a great little book called *The Desperate Gourmet* in the mid-1980s, regularly experimented with different styles of food that ended up on our dinner table. My dad even offered me a sip of his beer every now and then, but never coffee. Odd, now that I think about it, especially that I never even asked.

My first taste of coffee came after a fancy dinner at our neighbor's house on Englewood Road. The Steinschneiders, an older couple with grown children, occasionally invited our young family over to sit in the dining room for a meal. Mrs. Steinschneider made a big fuss over the after-dinner coffee, and I remember drinking a bit, loaded with milk and sugar, in a china cup.

I didn't drink coffee again until I sidled up to the coffee pot one morning as a desperate, newly ordained cleric at Old St. Paul's Church in downtown Baltimore, dumping in an embarrassing amount of sugar and cream. Basically, and I'm being honest and vulnerable here, my first foray into regular coffee drinking was an experience in warm coffee ice cream. As someone who now drinks his coffee the way he wears his clergy shirts—black—this admission is embarrassing.

It's not as if I'm addicted now or anything. Really. I just can't imagine getting the day kick-started without a mug of good coffee. Or making it through the afternoon for that matter.

Discovering the Good Stuff

Discovering Coffee Labs Roasters in Tarrytown, New York, sent me down the road to coffee snobbery. We lived in a neighboring town for seven years when I served All Saints' Church in Briarcliff Manor, about twenty miles up the Hudson River from New York City.

Not only did Coffee Labs roast all their own beans on site (so you left smelling great), not only did they offer free Wi-Fi (rare in those days), not only did they give free refills (exceedingly rare now),

Mike and Alicia Love at Coffee Labs Roasters in Tarrytown, NY.

they were also dog-friendly. For years I brought Delilah, our rescued yellow lab/husky mix, with me every Thursday morning as I wrote my sermon. Delilah would hang out with her best friend, a pug named Petunia, and I'd get down to business.

Granted, I was still drinking flavored coffee doctored up with cream and sugar (French vanilla!), but at least I was getting a taste of coffeehouse culture.

What finally cured me of flavored coffee was actually a physical that suggested I had slightly elevated cholesterol. This struck me as odd since I was running marathons back then and didn't eat, say, a stick of butter for breakfast. My solution revolved around getting rid of the cream. Thus: black coffee.

This epiphany coincided with a ten-day church retreat to a conference center in Mississippi. And it was there, in the rural Deep South, that I made the shift. I forced myself to drink that Mississippi mud, and by the time I came back home to "real" coffee, my cure had taken effect. Suddenly the flavors of the actual coffee burst through, and I realized what I had been missing all those years. Plus, I always had the nagging feeling the hip, tattooed and pierced baristas were quietly judging me and my flavored coffee as I doctored it up at the "fixin's bar."

As I learned about single-origin coffee and the differences between a cup of shade-grown Guatemalan coffee and coffee harvested from the Yirgacheffe region of Ethiopia, my Thursday morning sermon-writing ritual remained the same. Some churchgoers may need coffee to stay awake during the sermon. I need coffee to *write* the sermon and wouldn't dare subject anyone to the product of noncaffeinated sermon preparation. In fact, all the writing I do—books, blogs, sermons, articles—is both accompanied and enabled by coffee. I can't write anything without it. Well, I *can* but it's generally garbage.

For over fifteen years, I've spent Thursday mornings at coffee shops writing sermons. Some come easily and seem to flow directly from the caffeine into my brain and onto my laptop. Some involve gut-wrenching inner wrangling and external wrestling with the text over several cups of coffee. Most remain somewhere in between. But every week when I get up into the pulpit, for better or worse, coffee has played a major role in the words that come out of my mouth.

Seeking the Promised (Coffee) Land

My love affair with Coffee Labs, and owners Mike and Alicia Love, abruptly ended when my vocational life took me and my family to the Episcopal Parish of St. John the Evangelist in Hingham, Massachusetts, just south of Boston, in 2009. Leaving my beloved coffee shop and the community of writers and artists who frequented the place pained me. But surely, I thought, great coffee shops in metropolitan Boston must abound. It's the mecca of over-caffeinated college students! In my new town, I was delighted to note a coffee shop just down the street from the church called Brewed Awakenings. Great name, great location, but alas the coffee was terrible. Free Wi-Fi and great pastries cover a multitude of sins, but nothing can atone for lousy coffee.

Sure, I discovered some excellent coffee shops in Boston. Unfortunately, there were none on the South Shore. The wise men didn't search as diligently for the baby Jesus as I searched for a decent independent coffee shop within a ten-mile radius of Hingham. My working theory was that Dunkin' Donuts—the original store was a fifteen-minute drive to Quincy—had dumbed down everyone's coffee IQ to the point that no one even knew what good coffee tasted like. More "Dunkies" per capita exist on the South Shore than anywhere else in the free world. The problem is once you start drinking freshly roasted coffee from all over the world, the warm brown water served at Dunkin' Donuts just doesn't cut it. (I realize with that last statement, half of my own congregation has just tossed this book into Hingham Harbor.)

While still bemoaning the loss of Coffee Labs and trying out every coffee shop around to great disappointment, I was delighted one summer afternoon to encounter the Redeye Roasters truck at the Hingham Farmers Market. Sure, I wished he had an actual coffee shop, but Bob Weeks's coffee was outstanding, and he sold his own hand-roasted beans out of his mobile barista station. So I started stalking him. Every Saturday afternoon, my wife Bryna and I headed down to the farmer's market. I cared not a whit for the fresh produce. Green beans be damned, I showed up for Bob's *magic* beans and a made-to-order cup of freshly brewed single-origin coffee.

Eventually I got to know Bob and learned about his background as an advertising executive who gave it up in pursuit of the perfect cup of coffee. We're both evangelists in a way: he spreads the message of good coffee, and I share the good news of Jesus. But the real coup came when I approached him about the possibility of providing coffee for the church. I was hoping he might cut us a deal, but Bob took this further than I imagined and started donating freshly roasted beans to our congregation. He even helped me find and purchase a slightly used industrial-grade grinder, which I now consider one of the church's most prized and holy relics. Having fresh beans without a grinder would be like having the Bible without the ability to read.

This kept me drinking good coffee at home and at work, but I remained a coffee nomad when it came to my Thursday morning sermon-writing ritual. For two-and-a-half years, I felt like Moses and the Israelites wandering in the wilderness, seeking the elusive coffee-shop promised land. Finally, the miraculous happened. Mecca, to mix religious metaphors, arrived in Hingham. After years of urging, Bob opened Redeye Roasters Coffee & Espresso Lounge, giving coffee drinkers throughout the South Shore a destination artisanal coffee shop to call their own.

Drinking Coffee with Bob Weeks on the deck
of Redeye Roasters in Hingham, MA.

When Redeye opened in a former marina building overlooking Hingham Harbor, I was the third customer. (I would have been higher in the pecking order, but I had to take one of my kids to the pediatrician that morning.)

At its best, a coffee shop builds community. People gather to chat and plan and sip their favorite beverage and disagree and support one another and meet new people. Something magical happens that transcends our connections through social media and email and texting. Coffee brings people together, and Redeye Roasters has had that effect on our community. Selfishly, I was just glad to finally have a place to resume my Thursday-morning ritual within walking distance of the church. And it's where much of this book you're now holding has been written.

In the Beginning: Coffee Creation Stories

Coffee is the common man's gold, and like gold, it brings to every person the feeling of luxury and nobility.
　—Sheikh Abd-al-Kadir, sixteenth-century Muslim mystic

Most Americans don't associate their abundant coffee-drinking habits with Islam. If pressed to ponder coffee history, we might hearken back to the great coffeehouses of Europe or think about the tropical climates in which much of today's coffee is grown—Roman

Catholic strongholds like Brazil and other places in South and Central America. Many of us might even look to the Boston Tea Party as the reason we all drink coffee. Dump the tea! Stick it to the king! God bless America!

Despite the fact that Americans consume more coffee than any other country in the world, we know precious little about its history, let alone its deep religious roots. In an era of distrust among people of differing religious backgrounds, I love that we have Muslims to thank for discovering coffee. A shared coffee backstory offers an opportunity to see one another, especially those with whom we don't share a culture, with fresh eyes. Knowing that our common history binds us together and shines light upon our similarities rather than focusing on our differences reveals one of the true gifts of coffee culture.

Holy Dancing Goats!

When you take a sip of coffee, you drink in hundreds of years of history. And not just insipid, teacher-droning-on-endlessly-in-a-monotone history but a tale rich with thrilling stories that delight and inspire. It all begins with a wonderful, apocryphal account that involves ancient Muslims and dancing goats. Like most legends, it's been passed down for many years, and the precise origin is unclear.

At the center stands a young ninth-century Ethiopian goat herder named Kaldi. One day Kaldi took a short midday nap, as he was wont to do, and when he awoke, the goats in his care had disappeared. Panicked, he raced up the hill toward a clearing and observed something remarkable: the goats were dancing!

Upon closer inspection he noticed they were eating some bright red berries. Amazed, he stuck a handful in his pocket, regained control of his flock, and headed straight to the local monastery to share the miraculous story with the head monk.

Intrigued but dubious, the monk—well, let's let Faustus Naironi, the seventeenth-century Italian coffee historian, take it from here: "He resolv'd to try the virtues of these berries himself; thereupon, boiling them in water, and drinking thereof, he found by experience, it kept him awake in the night. Hence it happen'd, that he enjoin'd his Monastery the daily use of it, for this procuring watchfulness made them more readily and surely attend their devotions which they were obliged to perform in the night."[1]

Ripe coffee cherries growing on the vine in Nicaragua.

What I love about this story, besides the delightful image of dancing goats, is coffee's early connection to the prayer of the faithful. This community's first response to the effects of coffee beans was thanksgiving for diligence in prayer. And so, from the very beginning, a profound connection between coffee and faith emerged. Which doesn't atone for generations of lousy coffee served out of industrial-sized urns poured into Styrofoam cups in dank church basements, but it's a start.

Another delightful version of this story comes from the classic *All about Coffee*, written by William H. Ukers in 1922. After sharing a French translation of the legend, he concludes, "Piety does not exclude gastronomic instincts. Those of our good monk were more than ordinary; because he thought of drying and boiling the fruit of the herder. This ingenious concoction gave us coffee. Immediately all the monks of the realm made use of the drink, because it encouraged them to pray and, perhaps, also because it was not disagreeable."[2]

Not Disagreeable likely won't become the tagline for a major coffee brand, but anyone who has ever experienced that first sip of morning coffee could not, in fact, disagree with the sentiment.

Unfortunately, a few problems exist with the Kaldi story, including the fact that no monasteries existed in the Islamic world at the time. (Monks were considered unnatural since they rejected marriage and procreation.)

Nonetheless, it is generally agreed upon that coffee was first discovered in Ethiopia by devout Muslims who used it to enhance their prayer lives. I doubt many of us who faithfully begin each day with a cup of coffee think about the interfaith connections of that ritual.

They run deep, and regardless of religious tradition, we can all say "Amen!" to our cherished coffee ancestors.

Omar the Dervish

Just as Genesis contains not one but *two* creation stories (God creates the world in six days in the first chapter, and God creates Adam and Eve in the second), coffee lore also has two origin stories. In addition to Kaldi and his dancing goats, there's the story of Omar the Dervish.

Omar was a popular and respected Sufi healer, a member of the Shadhili sect of Muslims in the city of Mocha in Yemen (yes, that's where the term *mocha* comes from). His effectiveness in the use of both traditional medicine and prayer so irked the ruling authorities that they spread salacious rumors about him having an affair with the king's daughter, forcing him into exile in the nearby desert.

Omar soon found himself emaciated and starving to death when he happened upon a bush of red berries. Desperate for food, but believing it was a sign from God, Omar picked the bitter berries and ate them. In time, he built a fire, roasted the beans, put them in hot water, and drank the concoction. Suddenly fortified, Omar gained enough strength to sustain him for days.

Like the desert fathers and mothers of the early Christian tradition, people soon made pilgrimages to Omar's cave. He gave them his berry drink as medicine and quickly gained a popular following due to his miracle medicine. His supporters, seeing Omar's survival as a religious sign, appealed to the ruler to let him return to Mocha, which he did to great acclaim. Omar continued to promote coffee drinking, and it soon caught on with fellow Sufis, who boiled the grounds and drank them to keep alert and awake during their night prayers—similar to the religious community in the account of Kaldi.

We can't verify much about these two coffee creation stories. Yet, in the Christian tradition, the role of pious legend has long played a role in religious lore and devotion. All sorts of legends surrounding saints have arisen that, whether or not actually true, point to deeper truths that transcend our black-and-white notions of truth. Such is the case with the accounts of Kaldi's goats and Omar the Dervish.

These two stories also hint at the rather obfuscated history between coffee's discovery and its first consumption as a drink. Although coffee was discovered in Ethiopia, it was first cultivated in neighboring Yemen. Hence the two creation stories with one centered in Ethiopia and the other across the Red Sea in Yemen.

In the age of Kaldi, it's not as if the newly unearthed coffee beans suddenly propelled themselves into high-end espresso drinks. Like the goats, Ethiopians likely chewed the coffee cherries (the small fruit inside of which grow two beans) to get their buzz. Think of it as the energy-inducing PowerBar of the ninth century. It wasn't until the time of Omar that coffee was first consumed as a drink. He probably boiled water over an open fire, adding in some beans along with a few leaves from the coffee plant, which sounds disgusting but likely had an intoxicating effect.

What *is* true is this: historians and botanists agree that the genus *Coffea arabica* (what we know as the coffee plant) is indigenous to Ethiopia, where it continues to grow wild in some regions.

What's in a Name?

These days you need an advanced degree in linguistics to comprehend the typical menu at a decent coffee shop. From latte to cappuccino to macchiato to cortado to espresso, a whole range of insider language gets thrown around between baristas and discerning customers. And this is before deciphering the fake coffee vocabulary created by Starbucks. Whenever I find myself at one, usually when I'm desperate and in an airport, I take great pride in ordering a "medium black coffee," rather than using their pseudo-Italian jargon. "You mean a grande?" they ask. "Uh, no. I mean a medium." It's just my little way of sticking it to The Man. Never mind that the woman in front of me just ordered a triple, venti, half-sweet, nonfat, caramel macchiato.

Granted, all this lingo talk is rich coming from a member of the clergy. Around the altar, we don't use common terms for anything. A cup? No, it's a chalice. Oh, you think that's a plate? It's a paten. Robe? Ha. It's an alb. At its worst, this insider language confuses visitors and obscures the message. It does, however, set apart ritual objects as holy and special, and suddenly everyday items take on deeper meaning. Language matters and perhaps this coffee-shop vocabulary points to the often transcendent relationship we have with our coffee drinks.

Many etymologists believe the derivation of the word "coffee" comes from the name of the ancient Ethiopian kingdom of Kaffa, while others think it comes from the Arabic word *qahwa*, meaning *wine*. As Sufi mystics used coffee to aid prayer, perhaps even leading to a state of spiritual intoxication, the word evolved to refer to this new energy drink.

A legend cited by some scholars of Islam combines these two theories. It accepts that coffee was named for the region of Kaffa but also links it to *qahwah* as meaning *wanting no more*. This is based on several stories that link *kaffa* to the Arabic root for *it is enough*.

The tale begins with a religious man seeking to extend the Prophet's religion from the East toward West Africa. "And when he came into the regions where Kaffa lies, Allah is reported to have appeared to him and to have said, 'It is far enough, go no further.' Since that time, according to tradition, the country has been called Kaffa."[3] Naturally, the man immediately discovered a coffee tree with red berries which he boiled, drank, and named for the place Allah had led him.

Likely because of the *qahwa* connection, and coffee's effect, Europeans originally called coffee the "wine of Islam." Though the derivation of the English word has yet another layer, as the Turkish word *kahve* derived from the Arabic *qahwah* before being imported as *caffè* in Italian and finally *coffee* in English.

Another word for coffee in classical Arabic is *bunn*, a term of Ethiopian origin that refers to the bean itself. The tenth-century Persian physician Rhazes, credited with having written the earliest account of coffee's medicinal properties, used this label. In his work, he wrote of the coffee drink as *bunchum*, and one of his disciples, the physician known in the West as Avicenna (ibn Sina), wrote this about the healthful qualities of *bunn*: "It fortifies the members, it cleans the skin, and dries up the humidities that are under it, and gives an excellent smell to all the body."[4] Apparently coffee was the world's first deodorant.

Coffee Revealed to Muhammad

Although the stories of Kaldi and Omar serve as the earliest references to coffee, a legend exists that the archangel Gabriel himself revealed coffee to the prophet Muhammad. If you've ever been to a Christmas pageant, you'll remember Gabriel playing a prominent role in the nativity story (though I distinctly recall the year we didn't have enough boys so we ended up with the archangel Gabrielle).

Gabriel appears in the scriptures of all three Abrahamic faiths. In the Hebrew Bible, Gabriel explains Daniel's visions. In the Christian New Testament, Gabriel foretells the birth of both John the Baptist and Jesus in Luke's Gospel. And in Islamic tradition, Gabriel reveals the Qur'an to Muhammad and is referred to as the Angel of Revelation.

Evidently, according to coffee lore, Gabriel revealed more than just the holy book. One day, when the Prophet was not feeling well, Gabriel brought Muhammad a relief potion sent directly from Allah. The drink, said to have been as dark as the Holy Black Stone of Mecca, immediately revived Muhammad, allowing him to continue his holy work. Another source says a cup of brewed coffee was bestowed upon him before an important battle, giving him the stamina to unseat forty horsemen and possess fifty women.[5] Being that the prophet died in 632 and coffee wasn't discovered until the ninth century, this is difficult to verify.

This attempt by coffee drinkers in the Muslim world to retroactively gain the Prophet's blessing upon this new and controversial beverage also highlighted the near-exclusive patronage of coffeehouses by men.

Coffee Controversy!

Once its popularity spread beyond the local Sufi communities and hit the mainstream (apparently this took hundreds of years), questions about coffee began to emerge. When the Turks, under the aegis of the Ottoman Empire, conquered Yemen in the early sixteenth century, coffee culture exploded. As coffee moved beyond the world of religious ceremony, all sorts of legal and ethical questions arose, and the debate went right to the heart of Islamic religious life.

The acceptance of coffee in the Muslim world was by no means a foregone conclusion. Although the Qur'an forbids drinking alcohol, many Muslims turned to the well-known stimulating effects of coffee for energy and comfort. Some devout Muslim leaders saw coffee as an evil substitute for wine—an intoxicant used by the weak to subvert the alcohol ban but still become "intoxicated."

After coffee had spread to Mecca, a meeting of jurists held coffee up against the core beliefs of Islam. It was critical to examine what the Qur'an had to say about wine (*khamr*) and the idea that "every intoxicant is *khamr* and every intoxicant is forbidden," as it made people "incapable of distinguishing a man from a woman or the earth from the heavens." This was balanced against *jaziri ta' assub*, or the danger of an over-exaggerated piety.[6]

Coffee's partisans looked to a passage in the Qur'an that, they said, foretold coffee's use by followers of Muhammad: "They shall be given to drink an excellent wine, sealed; its seal is that of the musk."

Being for or against coffee literally and figuratively became one of the Muslim world's hottest topics as the Ottoman Empire reached the height of its power in the sixteenth century. Can you imagine being in a culture where people debated and fought over a beverage? Of course you can. You studied Prohibition and saw *The Untouchables* starring Robert De Niro as Al Capone.

In 1511, a squirrelly man named Kha'ir Bey served as governor of Mecca. One evening as he left the mosque following prayers, he witnessed a group of coffee drinkers heading into the mosque for their own evening devotions. Deeply offended (at first he thought they were drinking wine), he resolved to banish this exhilarating drink that he believed would lead citizens into great temptation in the holy city.

The following day he called together a council of leading citizens and government officials, described what he had seen, and called upon them to make coffee illegal. In the indictment against coffeehouses, it was declared, "In these places men and women met and played tambourines, violins, and other musical instruments. There were also people who played chess, mankala, and other similar games, for money; and there were many other things done contrary to our sacred law—may God keep it from all corruption until the day when we shall appear before him!"[7]

Now this sounds like great fun to me, though I could see how drinking coffee while someone banged a tambourine in my face could become irritating. Governor Bey's pronouncement caused widespread confusion in the community, however, as many were already avowed coffee drinkers. A hotly contested debate arose involving lawyers, physicians, and clerics, but in the end, the governor had his way. He announced a decree banning coffee, forbidding its sale, and closing the coffeehouses, and burned the remaining supply of beans.

Fortunately, the victory over coffee was short-lived. Once the decree reached the sultan, he lashed out at the governor for attempting to condemn something in Mecca already approved in Cairo, the kingdom's capital, and coffee quickly reestablished itself in the city. As for the governor? The following year he was accused of embezzlement, and the sultan sentenced him to death.

This isn't to say coffee was without controversy in Cairo—indeed the coffee controversy raged. The Ottoman emperor Selim I brought coffee to Egypt after conquering it in the early sixteenth century. In time, as coffeehouses became popular, a number of preachers saw them, and coffee itself, as a threat to their influence. Coffeehouses had a stronger appeal, in some cases, than their own houses of worship. Today's clergy can take solace in the realization that this phenomenon is nothing new.

The debate festered until 1534 when a fiery preacher railed against its consumption, believing it contrary to Islamic law and proclaiming coffee drinkers were not true Muslims. The congregation, adequately riled up, left worship, stormed a nearby coffeehouse, and set it ablaze. Suddenly all of Cairo was divided into two camps. The chief justice, a Solomon-like figure, brought the warring parties together, heard their arguments, and then ordered coffee served to both sides. This united the parties, and coffee became more popular than ever. I'm not sure about this as a mediation strategy, but apparently it worked in sixteenth-century Cairo.

The controversy over coffee among Muslims continued on throughout the sixteenth century and into the seventeenth century as well. Around 1560, Abd-Al-Qadir Al-Jaziri produced a manuscript titled *Umdat Al-Safwa* (Argument in Favor of the Legitimate

Use of Coffee), a response to the religious debates over the merits and legality, under Islamic law, of the increasingly popular drink sweeping the Muslim world. It remains the oldest existing document about the history, preparation, uses, virtues, and benefits of coffee drinking.

Still, the debates continued in ways that touched both religion and politics. Murad III, sultan of Istanbul from 1574 to 1595, had no problem murdering his entire family (he had his nine brothers strangled) in his quest to ascend the throne.[8] He did, however, have an issue with his subjects spending time in coffeehouses, perhaps because when they gathered, his cruelty was often the subject of conversation. Seeing the coffeehouse as a hotbed of sedition, Murad III banned them in 1580. The outward reason was religion, but the real reason was politics. And again, the ban didn't take.

The height of coffee persecution, and perhaps its last gasp, came under Sultan Murad IV (1623–1640). He was so intent on eradicating coffee from his kingdom, he made its consumption a capital offense. It's said that the sultan himself traveled in disguise around the streets of Istanbul and decapitated anyone seen drinking coffee.[9] Which sounds like an excellent plot for a historical horror movie. Still, coffee drinkers persisted, and the sultan's successors advocated leniency for the caffeine deprived.

Proponents of coffee used all their creative prowess to champion the drink they had fallen for. One example is the poem "In Praise of Coffee" written by Sheikh Abd-al-Kadir in 1587.

Oh coffee, you dispel the worries of the great,
you point the way to those who have wandered from
the path of knowledge. Coffee is the drink of the

friends of God, and of His servants who seek wisdom.

As coffee steeps in the cup it gives off a musky
aroma and turns the colour of ink. No one can understand
the truth until he drinks of its frothy goodness.
Those who condemn coffee as causing man harm are
fools in the eyes of God.

Coffee is the common man's gold, and like gold it
brings to every man the feeling of luxury and nobility.
Coffee differs from pure, gentle milk only in its taste
and colour.

Take time in your preparation of coffee and
God will be with you and bless you and your table.
Where coffee is served there is grace and splendour and
friendship and happiness.

All cares vanish as the coffee cup is raised to the
lips. Coffee flows through your body as freely as your
life's blood, refreshing all that it touches: look you at
the youth and vigour of those who drink it.

Whoever tastes coffee will forever forswear the liquor
of the grape. Oh drink of God's glory, your purity
brings man only well-being and nobility.[10]

In this poem, you see all the arguments of the day: how coffee is of
God, how only fools condemn it, how it transcends class, how it is
medicinal in its properties, and how it's the perfect antidote to wine.

In a clear demonstration of the drink's surging popularity, a covenant introduced into the marriage contract in Cairo bound husbands to keep an adequate supply of coffee in the home for the use of their wives. Failing to keep this covenant was grounds for divorce. So, while women could not drink in the coffeehouses, coffee was understood as a basic staple of their daily lives. Despite the patriarchy embedded in coffee history, which follows a similar pattern in culture, faith, and politics, this nod to parity in coffee consumption is striking. And, based on most of the women I know, live, and work with, coffee remains a cherished daily staple.

Despite all the controversy—and the reasons cited against coffee, including public safety, medical reasoning, and theology—the allure of coffee in the Muslim world remained strong. There were never any serious threats to its communal standing once coffee became established at Mecca and the debates settled. Not only was it incredibly popular, it also had tremendous social and economic effects. Once the java genie was released, no one stood a chance of forcing it back into the bottle.

Origin Tour

Should I kill myself, or have a cup of coffee?
—Albert Camus, twentieth-century French
philosopher and novelist

Before I started getting serious about coffee, I never thought about where this magic liquid came from. Everyone talks about coffee *beans*, sure. But I'm not a farmer, and my only experience with beans was picking up lima beans when I saw them on the grocery list. Coffee beans? Those are brown and come in bags. I had no idea how they grew. Underground? On a shrub? In a tree? Or how they were harvested. And I didn't really care. As long as my coffee got brewed in a timely fashion every morning, I was good.

After walking into some long-forgotten coffee shop and seeing pictures of farmers on the wall, it dawned on me that *someone* had to provide the coffee. Eventually I did some reading and googling, and that helped put things into perspective. I learned that coffee grows on small trees that produce "cherries" containing two coffee seeds, or beans. I also discovered there is a narrow tropical band around the equator where coffee grows. I couldn't just drop a few beans into the soil in my New England backyard and start drinking the bounty come spring. And even if I could, it takes three to four years before a coffee tree bears fruit.

In order to fully experience the coffee connection, I had to get myself to a coffee farm. So I contacted my old friends Mike and Alicia from Coffee Labs and asked if they knew any farms that might be willing to host a gringo who had made the brilliant decision to take French rather than Spanish in high school. It turns out Mike visits several farms every year, and he invited me to tag along with him on his trip to Nicaragua and El Salvador.

This was no watered-down agritourism. I entered into the very heart of the coffee industry, and I remain ever grateful for the opportunity to experience it firsthand. I met some incredible people along the way and learned just how many unseen hands touch the coffee that ends up in our cups.

Going to Origin

"Have you been to origin?" The first time a coffee geek asked me this question, I had no idea what she was taking about. Was *origin* a coffee-growing region in Brazil? A reference to my birthplace of

Milwaukee? In seminary I learned of an early Christian theologian named Origen—I didn't think that's what she meant.

When coffee folks refer to *origin*, they mean a coffee farm, as in where coffee originates. It's unstated, but if you're in the coffee industry and haven't been to origin, you're still a coffee virgin. Each trip

Mike and Dave insisted on pulling over on our way to the mountains for a photo op.

to another coffee-producing country adds another notch on a coffee stud's belt and allows for more caffeine-induced swagger.

Coffee roasters go to origin for a variety of reasons. It's an opportunity to form relationships with the farmers whose coffee is being purchased. It allows buyers to taste different coffees in a particular region to decide which ones they want to sell to customers back home. It plays an important role in educating consumers about the connection between individual farms and the coffee in their cup. The ability to speak with authority about specific coffee-growing regions is good marketing strategy. And it rekindles the passion for coffee that drove folks into the business in the first place.

Being awakened by a rooster at 5:00 a.m. in Nicaragua never made my bucket list. That's how the first full day on my trip to origin began. After flying into Managua and driving three hours into the mountainous Jinotega region, I was jazzed to visit my first ever coffee farm. I arrived with Mike, Dave MacIntyre (one of Coffee Labs' roasters), and our guide Francisco Javier Valle García. Mike and Dave are hard-charging, passionate coffee guys for whom quality coffee and having fun in the process is a lifetime pursuit.

Francisco, a native of Jinotega, and his family have been coffee farmers for generations. For five years he worked in Portland, Oregon, as a roaster for the high-end, specialty coffee company Stumptown before returning to Nicaragua to start a family and help transform the country's coffee culture. He now works with coffee farmers all over the coffee-producing regions, exporting specialty-grade coffee and matching farms with roasters seeking outstanding coffee.

Francisco is an exporter, but he's also something of a matchmaker and promoter of Nicaraguan coffee. Nicaragua is not the first country

Francisco Javier Valle García with the drying beds
at Expocamo, the mill he runs in Jinotega.

that comes to mind when thinking about coffee, but it produces
some outstanding beans. Like all coffee-producing countries, it also
grows a ton of crappy coffee that ends up in cans of Folgers or Chock
full o'Nuts. Excellent coffee only begins to grow at an elevation of

around 3,500 feet. Plenty of coffee farms, or *fincas*, exist in the lower altitudes; they just don't produce very good coffee. Passing large-scale processing plants on roads heading toward the mountains, you see bags of coffee stacked up outside, being damaged by the sun.

Francisco made for a gracious host and eager guide, proud to show off the best of Nicaraguan coffee farmers and their operations. He runs a coffee mill called Expocamo, where farmers bring their freshly picked and washed coffee to be processed. Francisco determines its quality and price before exporting the beans to roasters all over the world.

It's true that you never forget your first coffee farm. Mine was Finca Buena Vista in the mountains of Nicaragua, five hours north of Managua on the Honduran border. The last hour of the trip, which we took in a bright red Toyota pickup truck driven by the farmer, Ronny Herrera, took place on a winding, single-lane dirt road, which makes it awkward when another vehicle comes barreling down the mountain. The last ten minutes of the drive felt particularly harrowing, but the vistas, as the name of the farm suggests, were stunning.

The first thing you notice at a coffee farm is the topography. The trees, which stand around six or seven feet tall—basically really large shrubs—get planted at obscenely steep grades up and down the sides of the mountain. One wrong step and you'll end up in the valley below. Bram de Hoog, an engaging young Dutchman who worked with Francisco, told me that just the week before he had lost his footing and tumbled thirty feet down the mountain. Yikes!

In the end, no one goes to origin solely for bragging rights. It completes the circle for people passionate about the end result of a beautiful cup of coffee. Jesus said, "I am the Alpha and the Omega, the beginning and the end." If origin is the alpha, the roaster is the omega. From farm-to-cup marks the beginning and the end.

One of my favorite moments visiting coffee farms in Central America took place at lunch with Mike and the farmers, following a tour of Finca El Paraiso outside of Santa Ana in El Salvador. (The symbolism of a clergyman visiting a place that translates as Paradise Farm wasn't lost on me.) Mike had not previously visited this particular farm, though he had been roasting their coffee for several years. As we walked through the fields, up and down some steep paths, the pride taken by everyone involved came bursting through. The loving care they put into tending to each tree—the pruning and fertilizing—is astounding. They pour their hearts into what is very difficult, labor-intensive work that still exists to a large extent at the whim of weather conditions.

At lunch, Martin, the farm's longtime supervisor, a short and intense man who spends his days with a machete strapped to his side, hesitantly asked Mike about the coffee's quality. He knows what it looks like on his end, at origin. But there was something quite vulnerable sounding in his question. It reminded me of John the Baptist's question to Jesus after John's imprisonment. He sent his disciples to ask Jesus, "Are you the one who is to come, or are we to wait for another?" (Matthew 11:3). In other words, has my whole life's purpose as the forerunner of the Messiah been in vain? He's pretty sure he knows the answer, but still, he seeks confirmation from the only person who can authentically answer the question about Jesus's identity—Jesus himself.

In the same way, Martin the supervisor, in questioning Mike, was asking the only person who could authentically answer the question about his coffee's quality. Mike assured Martin that he grew outstanding coffee and communicated, through our guide and interpreter, Gabriela Flores, just how much he appreciates their team's continued commitment to quality. For Martin, Mike's affirmation offered a glimpse beyond his world into the side of the coffee industry he cannot see in his day-to-day life.

This parallels what it must be like when your favorite barista or roaster finally gets to go to origin. They see the side of the coffee process that has long existed only in theory. Without experiencing origin, there exists a blind spot—not for lack of interest but for lack of proximity. On both sides of the growing/roasting continuum, the fullness of the coffee cycle is literally a world away. For people of faith, proximity to the divine offers meaning and context; in the coffee world, proximity invites similar perspective and connection to the bigger picture.

I'm Just a Bean

As a kid, I loved the *Schoolhouse Rock* introduction to how a bill got passed into law. Sure, "I'm Just a Bill" was an annoying interruption to *The Flintstones*, but it had a catchy tune and beat watching yet another ad for Hasbro's Hungry Hungry Hippos.

You can think about the transition of coffee from plant to roasted bean in the same way. A number of steps must take place to exact the beautiful transformation, and visiting a coffee farm and a coffee mill provided me the education.

Coffee doesn't begin life as a bean. As a fruit, the coffee plant produces cherries that grow in bunches, and the first time I ate a dark red, ripe coffee cherry plucked directly off the vine, the sheer sweetness astonished me. It's like eating a soft, sugary cherry, but instead of a pit, two coffee seeds (the precious beans!) nestled inside emerged covered in a slimy substance called mucilage.

Unfortunately for coffee pickers, the cherries do not ripen uniformly, necessitating multiple passes to collect the ripe cherries during harvest season, which varies from country to country depending on geography and proximity to the equator. The coffee at the highest elevations, which is also the best coffee, ripens last—well after the commodity-grade stuff.

After a seasonal worker picks the ripe cherries, the cherries are gathered together, bagged, and taken to the mill. Before the green-colored beans can be exported as coffee, the fruit surrounding the beans must be removed. This is the first step in processing coffee. While some large farms have their own mills on site, small farmers, who make up the vast majority of coffee growers in most countries, take their picked cherries to a regional mill.

In order to get to the beans while preserving the coffee's complex flavor, a prescribed process takes place at the mill. Processors use one of two systems to remove the husk and pulp from ripe coffee cherries: the wet method or the dry method.

In the dry, or natural, method, the cherries are laid out on elevated drying sheets or on open patios. Workers rake them regularly over the next two weeks, rotating the cherries so they don't get spoiled, until the beans can be easily removed by hand or machine.

In the wet method, a more modern process, the cherries first pass through a floater tank. At this stage, you'll hear coffee folks refer to floaters—that's a bad thing. Conveniently enough, the good, healthy cherries sink while defective or diseased cherries float. After this, the remaining good cherries are routed through a depulping machine, which removes the skin, known as cascara. Then the beans, including their parchment and mucilage, spend time in fermentation tanks for twelve to forty-eight hours, before being dried in the sun.

Regardless of method, the end product is known as *parchment coffee* because the individual beans retain a light layer of skin. The parchment coffee gets bagged and stored in warehouses until it is ready for export. At this point, the coffee is hulled by a machine that removes the parchment and is graded and sorted according to quality and size. The final step before bagging the beans for export is removing defective beans—either by hand or machine.

I didn't realize that the word *bodega* simply means warehouse in Spanish. Imagine my surprise when I entered a building labeled *bodega* expecting to see a New York City–style convenience store selling scratch-off lottery tickets and instead encountered 152-pound bags of coffee piled up to the ceiling. It's an impressive sight for a coffee lover, one that evokes phrases like "lifetime supply" and "kingdom of heaven." Entering a coffee warehouse gives you a sense of the scale of both the operation at hand and the industry as a whole.

Coffee Pickers

No one thinks much about the pickers, the unsung heroes of the entire operation. Pickers sit at the bottom of the coffee chain economically and socially, yet if the coffee isn't picked when perfectly ripe, the lack of flavor will show in the cup.

Picking coffee is difficult, treacherous work, and seeing the terrain upon which they must labor reminded me of the origin story of Kaldi and his goats. They must have been *mountain* goats because the balance required to pick coffee cherries with a large basket tied to your waist in places where one wrong step could lead to serious injury or even death—and let's face it, there's no workers' comp—stunned me. I had trouble just keeping my balance walking through some of the trees, and I wasn't on the steepest grades trying to quickly pick the ripe cherries all day in the hot sun.

Pickers generally get paid by the weight of the cherries they pick, so the best and most efficient pickers receive the most money. Some pickers live locally near the farms, while others are migratory and

It takes many hands to pick coffee during harvest season

go where there is work. Some families work together with children picking as well. While child-labor abuses are an issue in some countries, in many cases it's simply a matter of keeping families together. In other words, if both mom and dad spend the day working in the fields, kids tagging along becomes a form of childcare. In most coffee-producing nations, school vacations intentionally revolve around the picking season.

During harvest season, unless their homes are nearby, coffee pickers live on the farm, often in primitive bunk-style shelters. The one I peeked into had three levels of wooden bunks and housed about fifty workers. It was hot, smelly, dark, and primitive. There were no mattresses, blankets, or pillows, and certainly no privacy, running water, or electricity.

The pickers remain the most vulnerable population in the coffee industry. In Nicaragua, pickers earn as little as $2 or $3 dollars per day even though the minimum wage is officially $6. The specialty coffee farms I visited paid between $7 and $10 per day, but that's the high end.

One of the biggest issues for pickers remains the working conditions. Besides the inherent dangers of mountaintop coffee picking, pickers supply their own equipment, such as boots and rain gear, which are often inadequate to the task at hand. The major health hazard on some farms involves not being provided with proper protection when applying dangerous pesticides. But at least coffee pickers in Nicaragua no longer have to carry weapons with them, as murals depict from the war-torn days of the Sandinista revolution.

Some farmers genuinely do seek to improve the lives of those who work on their farms. At Finca El Paraiso, the woman whose family has owned the land for four generations cares deeply for those who live and work on or near the farm. While Claudia Mathies de Rank was away tending to a sick relative, her husband, Federico, told me of her passion especially for the children of the pickers. In addition to a library in the workers' housing area, she recently had a computer lab installed. She also pays for medical clinics to make regular visits to the area, helping not only families who work for her but those in the broader community as well. As Federico put it, "What's good for the community is good for the farm."

Claudia's grandmother had a small church built on the property in the 1940s, and weekly services still take place there, even as it is increasingly rare to find a priest to say mass. I toured this church, called St. María Auxiliadora (which translates as Mary, Help of Christians) and one particular detail struck me: a statue of an obscure saint for most Westerners but a beloved figure in South and Central America. Saint Martin de Porres (1579–1639), who spent his entire life in Peru, existed as a man on the margins as both a person of color and the illegitimate son of a freed slave and a Spanish nobleman. A Dominican monk known for his ministry to the hopeless and the helpless, Martin tirelessly served the poor and forgotten. In iconography and statuary, Martin is often depicted holding a broom, signifying his humility and willingness to see any task, no matter how menial, as an act of sacred service. There may not officially be a patron saint of coffee pickers, but I think Martin de Porres would be the perfect choice.

Coffee Supply Chain

Mike Love tells the story of a coffee farmer he knew who one year came to visit him in New York. The farmer loved seeing the end of the cycle where the coffee he had so faithfully and lovingly tended ends up in the cup of consumers. Mike set aside an evening at the shop for customers to meet the farmer, ask questions, and learn about the rarely seen, mysterious front-end of the coffee industry.

Things were going well until the farmer noticed the 12-ounce bags of his coffee being sold on a shelf near the counter. He started getting agitated and pulled Mike aside. The gist being, "You're selling this bag of my coffee for $17 and you only paid me $4? You're ripping me off!" Mike took a deep breath, knowing the inevitability of the conversation, and sat down with the farmer to explain all of his costs and assure him that his own profit on the bag being sold equaled the farmer's profit. All was well, and the great relationship between Mike and this farmer of incredible coffee continues to this day.

So where does the rest of the money go? The journey from coffee plant to coffee cup is long and serpentine. The coffee in your morning cup has passed through many more hands than you'd imagine. The first one to touch it is the farmer who grew it, but that's just the beginning of the journey. Whether the coffee you're drinking was grown in Colombia, Honduras, Yemen, Vietnam, or Hawaii, a number of steps occur before it becomes the liquid gold we all crave.

After processing, most coffee ends up on container ships, which translates into transportation, insurance, freight, and inspection fees. Once the ship arrives in the destination port, customs fees and

With Mike Love of Coffee Labs Roasters and a coffee tree at Finca Buena Vista in northern Nicaragua.

additional inspection costs accrue before the beans are transported to an importer or trader's warehouse. Finally, the coffee arrives at the roastery, which may or may not be the same entity as the coffee shop where they will be ground and brewed by a skilled barista. Rent and Global North labor make up a significant portion of the coffee-shop owner's costs.

At first glance, the injustice of a coffee picker earning $7 per day while a Global North consumer pays $3 for a cup of coffee seems inconceivable. Awareness of how you spend your coffee dollar and the impact it makes on people up and down the supply chain remains the responsibility of every consumer who cares about the lives of others, and it's an issue we'll explore in a later chapter.

In the end, this is what makes a trip to origin so valuable. It allows the hidden stories of people in the coffee industry to be shared with consumers who will never walk up and down the hillsides of a subtropical coffee-growing region. So many lives and so many stories and so many people exist behind the to-go cup you grab on your way to catch the train or pick up your kids or meet a friend. Beyond the visible world of our own experience, life is teeming with activity. The wide world of coffee reminds us that our needs do not, in fact, stand at the center of the universe. And that connections exist, whether seen or unseen, between our lives and those who farm, mill, and enjoy coffee all over the world.

Coffee and Prayer

It is inhumane, in my opinion, to force people who have a genuine medical need for coffee to wait in line behind people who apparently view it as some kind of recreational activity.

—Dave Barry, humorist and writer

When I first started writing this book, I was clear about one thing: it would not be a cheesy devotional guide that delved into "sip deeply and reflect upon the state of your soul." I have certainly experienced transcendent moments in my life while drinking coffee; times when prayer and coffee blended together in magical ways. I'm all for pouring a cup of coffee and navel-gazing—occasionally. I just had no desire to write about it.

Many coffee drinkers, regardless of creed, have claimed religious experiences through coffee. Hang around specialty coffee folks long enough and you'll hear the expression "God in a cup." It's the title of Michaele Weissman's classic 2008 coffee book. With the subtitle *The Obsessive Quest for the Perfect Coffee*, Weissman follows several coffee-industry hot shots around the world in a passionate search for the greatest coffee on earth. It's a rollicking tale of adventure, intrigue, and larger-than-life personalities.

When I first spotted the book on Amazon, I thought "Oh, great. Another insipid book about coffee and spirituality." After reading the description, though, I became intrigued about the title. It's derived from a characterization of one of the finest, and most expensive, coffees in the world. The coffee, Hacienda La Esmeralda Special from Panama, elicited the remark during a competition that is essentially a beauty pageant for high-end coffee. It was uttered by Don Holly, the quality-control manager at Green Mountain Coffee in Vermont, who, upon tasting it for the first time, declared that he "saw the face of God in the cup."

The comment was not an overtly religious one—Don has said publicly he's not a particularly religious man—but it revealed the transcendent possibilities of coffee. As a person of faith, I believe God can be found in all manner of things and circumstances. In a cup of coffee, in a passing interaction with a stranger, in times of celebration, in moments of adversity.

If prayer is ultimately about connection with God, then drinking coffee can surely be prayerful. We've witnessed the ancient association between coffee and prayer. In exploring the prayerful roots of what many consider to be the nectar of the gods, we affirm that God infuses more than religious rites. We proclaim that the face of God may indeed be revealed in a cup of coffee.

The Sufi Connection and Whirling Dervishes

As we've seen, Sufi Muslims share a direct link to the history of coffee. Sufism is often referred to as Islamic mysticism and is not a distinct sect, as it exists across both Sunni and Shia forms of Islam. Rather, it focuses on the purification of the inner self and the quest for direct experience of God.

While communities of Sufis form around grand masters known as *mawlas*, they consist of everyday people who come together for ritual practices. In this sense, they mirror congregations rather than monastic orders since they meet in specific places for their spiritual sessions. This important distinction likely provides a clue to the spread of coffee's popularity. As most practitioners of Sufism had regular jobs, their exposure to coffee in worship eventually left the spiritual context, moving into the household and ultimately to the coffeehouse.

Attaining *ihsan*, or "perfection of worship," serves as the Sufi's primary goal, and they look to the Prophet Muhammad as the perfect man who best exemplifies and embodies the morality of God.

The Sufi mystic and theologian Shaikh ibn Isma'il Ba Alawi declared that coffee, when imbued with prayerful intent and devotion, could bring the believer to the experience of *qahwa ma'nawiyya*, or "the ideal *qahwa*," and *qahwat al-Sufiyya*, terms both meant to convey "the enjoyment which the people of God feel in beholding the hidden mysteries and attaining the wonderful disclosures and the great revelations."[1]

Ritual and prayer and coffee all came together in early Sufi communities. One sixteenth-century writer, Ibn ʿAbd al-Ghaffar, described the coffee ceremony among the Yemeni Sufis at Azhar: "They drank it every Monday and Friday eve, putting it in a large vessel made of red clay. Their leader ladled it out with a small dipper and gave it to them to drink, passing it to the right while they recited one of their usual formulas, mostly 'There is no god but God, the Master, the Clear Reality.'"[2]

While several accounts of this ceremony from various sources exist, they all mention the red vessel. The color had special meaning in Sufi worship, symbolizing the mystical union with God, the goal of their spiritual practice.

The Sufi whirling dervishes, perhaps aided by coffee, became famous for their twirling practice of prayer as a method for attaining ecstatic and mystical union with God. Founded by the Turkish poet and mystic Mevlana Jalaluddin Rumi (1207–1273)—the same Rumi of the incessantly shared quotes on Facebook—this active form of prayer continues to this day, although it's more commonly performed as a dance for tourists than used as a devotional practice.

Everything in the dance, known as the *Sema*, is imbued with symbolism. The camel-hair fez represents the tombstone of the ego; the black cloak a grave that, when removed, signifies the dancer's spiritual rebirth into the truth; the white skirt symbolizes the ego's shroud. Ultimately the *Sema* signifies submission to and unity with God.

If you've ever seen the whirling dervishes in action (check out YouTube videos if Istanbul isn't in your travel plans), you can understand the benefits of coffee consumption, even if you have no clue how they don't simply get dizzy and fall on their faces. Seriously, if you've ever been on the Tilt-A-Whirl at Six Flags and nearly threw up, this may not be your ideal spiritual practice.

But coffee most clearly identifies with the form of prayer known as *dhikr*. These nightly prayer sessions serve as an integral part of Sufi spirituality, as the name of Allah or a snippet of prayer or a verse from the Qur'an is repeated over and over again as a mantra. Through this meditative practice, the belief in the unity of Allah penetrates the heart.

In this vein, one early Sufi devotional ritual involved coffee-drinking accompanied by recitation of a *ratib*, the invocation 116 times of the divine name *Ya Qawi*, "O Possessor of All Strength!"[3]

The energizing effects of coffee were the perfect prayer partner for these mystics, and the drink became intrinsically linked to their *dhikr* sessions. Coffee did not serve as a sacramental or holy drink for the Sufis who popularized its use, but its discovery was considered a special blessing in its role as an aid to prayer.

In time, coffee's use spread to Mecca where, as the coffee historian Al-Jaziri notes, "It was drunk in the Sacred Mosque itself, so that there was scarcely a *dhikr* or *mawlid* [the observance of Muhammad's birthday] where coffee was not present."[4]

Morning (Coffee) Devotions

We've learned that not everyone was thrilled with the Sufis' use of coffee in their religious ceremonies. Then again, not everyone has always appreciated *my* use of coffee during prayer services. I will often drink my first morning cup of coffee while praying the daily office out of *The Book of Common Prayer*. Morning prayer and coffee just seem to go together, one ritual informing and amplifying another.

Once, very early on as a priest in a new congregation, while sipping coffee and saying the office with a few parishioners, an irate fellow worshipper accused me of "defaming prayer." She wasn't interested in my explanation of the long history of entwinement between coffee and prayer. It's not as if I was being obviously distracting about it during the informal gathering: "The Lord [sluuuuuurp] be with you." It was more take-a-sip-during-the-really-long-passage-from-Deuteronomy-that-someone-else-was-reading.

Granted, it wasn't really about the coffee. I later learned she had hoped and fervently prayed for another minister, one she knew, to be called to lead the parish. A few days after the coffee conflict, she found me in the hallway and declared, "I hate the words that come out of your mouth, your heart, and your *soul*." All I could think to say in response, after taking a sip of my coffee, was, "Well, that pretty much covers it."

At divinity school, worship provided an anchor that grounded each day in prayer. At Seabury-Western Theological Seminary in Evanston, Illinois, I came to love the rhythm of the thrice daily worship—morning prayer, Eucharist, and evening prayer. For the first time, I understood the attraction to the monastic lifestyle as the bells rang three times before each liturgy, summoning the faithful to worship. Whatever your day brought—studying, sleeping, conversing with a classmate about early church heresies, you dropped everything to enter the sacred space of the seminary chapel.

One of my good friends, Ann Johnson, now serving as pastor of a congregation in Connecticut, always arrived to morning prayer just after the opening acclamation. She'd rush in by a side door, hair still dripping wet, clutching her mug of coffee, ready to greet the day with coffee and prayer. Her faith in both coffee and morning worship still inspires me, and I always smile and think about Ann's dogged devotion as I sip my coffee and say my prayers. Also, she didn't hate my soul.

Nocturnal Rituals

In the Christian tradition, the concept of vigils runs deep. During the early days of the church, the all-night liturgy that preceded daybreak on Easter morning served as the most sacred ritual of the year and the Easter Vigil remains the most ancient of Christian liturgical rites.

I personally would have little chance at staying awake for Midnight Mass on Christmas Eve, let alone preaching a coherent sermon, without the aid of coffee. Yet, for as much emphasis as Christians have traditionally put on vigils, those celebrations that mark the eve of a great feast, coffee hasn't played a formal role. There's no vesting ritual that involves coffee, for instance. Although at one parish I served, a major coffee stain dotted the white clergy stole that matched the church's altar hangings. It happened before my time—no doubt one of my predecessors had a little accident while preparing for the early service on Sunday morning. Strangely, every time someone commented on this stain (it clearly wasn't sacramental wine), and I explained it didn't happen on my watch, they never believed me.

While vigils play a less important role in Judaism, there exists a midnight rite called *Tikkun Chatzot*, or the Rectification of Midnight. According to the Talmud, the central text of Jewish law and theology, God mourns the destruction of the temple in the dark of the night—a recognition of the depth and darkness of exile in relation to the light of daybreak.

This special nighttime service brought the worshipper into union with God's sorrow and, through repentance and prayer, conveyed hope that the temple would be rebuilt. While observed in various forms throughout the Middle Ages, the service never really caught on with the faithful. Some devout Jews even sought to move the service of *Tikkun* to an earlier hour.

It wasn't until the late sixteenth century that the service suddenly took off in Palestine and spread to other Jewish communities. Obviously, this beautiful liturgy only went viral because coffee appeared on the scene.[5] Once coffee became commonplace in the Jewish community, and Jews no longer struggled to stay awake, the issue of the earlier time slot became moot.

Ranger Pudding

While coffee has helped me stay alert during early morning devotions and the occasional late-night liturgy over the years, I don't pull many all-night prayer vigils. Unlike those first coffee-drinking Muslims or even *Tikkun*-praying Jews, I'm content to say the Lord's Prayer before bed, get a good night's sleep, and live to pray another day.

But I can relate to using coffee to stay awake and alert when all you want to do is give in to those visions of sugar plums dancing in your head. Sometimes you find yourself in situations where it takes superhuman effort to remain conscious.

When I was in the army we trained hard, and our tactical exercises often took place at night. I'd find myself lying prone with my weapon at the ready, set up in a perimeter waiting for another unit to try and penetrate our lines. Since much of my training occurred in New England, it was usually frigid. With the ground half-frozen, my toes and fingers would start to go numb. In the eerie quiet, my eyes would play tricks on me in the moonlight, and I'd hear all sorts of sounds—animals, the wind, perhaps a twig being snapped in two. My senses were heightened as I waited for the imminent attack while adrenaline coursed through my body. I embodied the epitome of the alert soldier, ready for anything.

But the longer I waited, the less alert I became. I'd start telling myself that it was just a war game, and no one would actually get hurt. My defenses would come down, the sleep monster would grab hold of me, and my eyelids would droop. I'd shake myself awake and with renewed vigor I'd keep watch. Until the minutes started to again slip by and I'd find myself in that "the-spirit-is-willing-but-the-flesh-is-weak" mode. That's when I'd suddenly remember the remedy to my ills: Ranger Pudding.

If you know anything about modern combat food, and I hope you don't, you're familiar with MREs. Soldiers take these prepackaged Meals Ready to Eat (also known as Meals Rejected by Everyone) with them out into the field. Each MRE contains a packet of powdered chocolate. To make Ranger Pudding, you'd rip off the top of the powdered chocolate, pour in the powdered coffee, the sugar, the creamer, add a bit of water from the canteen and then mix it all together until something resembling the consistency of thick mud emerged. Eat that, and the combined caffeine/sugar high kept you going through the night.

In my case, Ranger Pudding proved especially effective as I wasn't a coffee drinker and hadn't yet built up any immunity to caffeine. At all. A few bites of Ranger Pudding left me good to go for the duration. Of course, the taste was repulsive, but as Mary Poppins would say, "a spoonful of sugar helps the medicine go down." And that's precisely how I treated this concoction.

This must have been something like what those early coffee users experienced. They, too, had a mission: to stay awake for their night prayers. Vigilance mattered among the faithful. I'm not sure how the head of their faith community would have handled a young monk who dozed off during worship, but you certainly didn't want some crusty old sergeant finding you asleep out on the perimeter. And so this instant coffee mixture was indeed a godsend.

Mountaintop Experiences

Google *coffee and prayer* and nineteen million hits come up. It's hard to know which is more popular, but together they pack a powerful punch. Only a few million of these posts come from pastors sharing photos on Instagram of their recently ordered lattes with the Bible open to an underlined passage and the caption "Fueled by coffee and Jesus." For some reason, their Bibles are never open to the passage where Jesus says, "Beware of practicing your piety before others."

It's true Jesus never hung out at coffee shops, but he did regularly spend time apart in prayer. The whole concept of the mountaintop experience? He invented it. Coffee is the perfect companion for spending time in prayer, for "wasting time with God" as my favorite definition of prayer puts it. Coffee invites contemplation and introspection and the time apart that we all crave but that feels so elusive. There's just something about holding a warm mug of coffee that also warms the soul.

Whenever I take a sip of coffee while contemplating life and faith, I feel deeply connected to the ancient Muslims who first paired coffee with prayer. You can't help but be drawn spiritually closer to your sisters and brothers of all faiths who continue this practice across the globe. In ways both humbling and transcendent, it reminds me of my insignificance in the vast context of humanity, while also connecting me to something much larger.

It's not a bad metaphor for faith in general. For we are of infinite worth in God's eyes, valued and loved as unique manifestations of the divine, yet we do not stand as isolated beings in a detached universe. God's presence and the interconnectedness of humanity lift us up as valuable creatures even as we remain, ultimately, of little account in the grand scheme of global history.

I hesitate to use the word *mindfulness* here since I'm not big fan of the whole mindfulness movement. It's not that I think mindfulness is a bad thing—it's essential to an integrated, authentic, fulfilling life. But the commodification of the concept bothers me, and I automatically tune out when ideas become trendy. Plus, mindfulness seems to just be a rebranding of ancient concepts that exist in most Eastern and Western religions.

There persists, though, an opportunity for a fleeting moment of prayerfulness in that first cup of coffee—a chance to soak in the aroma as we soak in the presence of God. This doesn't work all the time, of course. We race out of the house to catch the commuter rail or we engage in the contact sport of wrangling kids out the door and onto the school bus. Some days the only prayer you manage to say over your coffee pot is, "Dear God, hurry the hell up!" There's little that's mindful in the madness of much of our lives.

But then there are the other days. The ones where we do have an extra moment to turn down the volume of our lives and enjoy fleeting solitude and silence. Maybe this is mindfulness. It certainly allows a moment of perspective and prayer and connection with forces beyond the visible world and offers us the opportunity to revel in the joyful gift of this beautiful drink.

Satan's Drink: Coffee and Christianity

Without my morning coffee I'm just like a dried up piece
of roast goat.
　　—Johann Sebastian Bach in his "Coffee Cantata," 1735

Initial resistance among the three Abrahamic faiths—Judaism, Christianity, and Islam—recurs as a theme in coffee's interaction with religion. In a sense, this mimics human nature's resistance to change. Faith demands we face and overcome fears and suspicions of things that take us out of our comfort zones. For beer-swilling Europeans of the Middle Ages, this new, dark, bitter drink from the land of

55

infidels was suspect. The story of Christianity's initial dance with coffee mirrors such resistance and presents an equal number of delightful stories and legends that accompany our continuing journey.

Coffee and the Crusades

While we rightly and roundly condemn the Crusades as a dark period in the history of the Christian church, they did affect the spread of coffee. This lone bright spot won't bring singing "Onward, Christian Soldiers" back into vogue, but following routes established by crusaders to the Holy Land, merchants began to trade in otherwise unknown or exceedingly rare commodities in the West.

But first, a touch of background to place this disturbing era into context. What became known as the Crusades began in 1095 when Pope Urban II encouraged European Christians to take up arms and fight Muslims in the Holy Land. The idea, which the First Crusade accomplished in 1099, was to capture Jerusalem and set up a Roman Catholic state.

Various internal disagreements threatened the alliance between the Latin crusaders and the Eastern Byzantine Christians, though they kept things together in order to take Constantinople and set up four crusader states. These held until the 1130s when the Muslims, declaring a Holy War, or *Jihad*, against these states began making inroads against the Christians.

This development led to the Second Crusade in 1147, which the unified Muslim forces soundly turned back, despite it being the largest force of crusaders to that point. Things went back and forth into the thirteenth century (historians count seven periods of crusade), with the Muslims continuing to gain strength and territory.

In the end, the Crusades had a number of unseemly consequences. These included greater schism between the Western and Eastern churches, increased enmity between Christians and Muslims, and demonization of Jews, which fueled anti-Semitism. The system of indulgences that helped spur the Protestant Reformation largely resulted from the church's need to fund the Crusades' military operations. Basically, the whole concept was a disaster, save for creating loads of fodder for future Dan Brown-inspired conspiracy theories.

On a positive note, at least for our purposes, sugar, spices, dates, apricots, and coffee were introduced on a much broader scale into Europe due to new trade routes. These were viewed as exotic foods, generally available only to the wealthy classes, and soon became symbols of status in the countries they were imported into. Many of the returning crusaders themselves returned with a taste for the items that became staples of their diets while abroad, though as far as coffee was concerned, the flow into Europe was barely a trickle at this point.

While the interaction between divergent cultures led, eventually, to some positive outcomes, it came at horrific human cost, and Christians ceded much moral authority in the endeavor.

Satan's Brew

Coffee first journeyed to the West in a sustained manner via early seventeenth-century Arab traders in Venice. The exotic new quaff was initially used for medicinal purposes before being marketed to and enjoyed by the city's wealthiest citizens. Despite its popularity and rapid growth—among the masses and with the opening of the first Venetian coffeehouse in 1645—coffee met significant resistance from more conservative forces in the Roman Catholic Church.

Once again, religious authorities sought to stop coffee's popularity, viewing it as an evil potion—ironically, now because of its association with Islam!

One legend involves Pope Clement VIII (1536–1605). As coffee consumption moved from Venice to Rome, a certain faction of priests at the Vatican denounced coffee as an invention of Satan and sought to have coffee banned. As William Ukers dramatically describes in *All about Coffee*, "They claimed that the Evil One, having forbidden his followers, the infidel Moslems, the use of wine— no doubt because it was sanctified by Christ and used in the Holy Communion—had given them as a substitute this hellish black brew of his which they called coffee. For Christians to drink it was to risk falling into a trap set by Satan for their souls."[1] In other words, this liquid heresy had no place among faithful Christians.

The pope, not wanting to make an ill-informed pronouncement, had some coffee prepared and brought to him. It is said that he then anointed coffee as a beverage for all Christians, reportedly declaring "Why, this Satan's drink is so delicious that it would be a pity to let the infidels have exclusive use of it. We shall fool Satan by baptizing it and making it a truly Christian beverage."

Whether or not this papal exchange actually took place is debatable, but the parallels between the early disputes over coffee in the Muslim and Christian worlds are striking and serve as windows into human nature. Some resist, some embrace, but in time life moves on.

With Bryna, searching for coffee at the Vatican.

In this case, the coffee momentum was unstoppable, and the beverage's blessing by the religious authorities, either in the moment or retroactively, eased the transition.

On a recent trip to Rome, I decided to commune with this coffee-loving pope by tracking down his grave. Ditching my family in some forgotten trattoria, along with our friends Harry, Andrea, and Madelaine Register, who joined us on this Italian adventure, I embarked upon my quest. In the stunning Basilica di Santa Maria Maggiore, I zipped past the fifth-century mosaics, relics of Saint Jerome, and Bernini statues to find the memorial to the first coffee-drinking pope. The side chapel that held his grave was locked. Rats! But I stuck my iPhone in between the iron bars to snap a picture of the statue marking Clement's grave. His right arm extended in a gesture of blessing that I'm pretty sure could have held a coffee cup.

In the story of papal blessing, we also see echoes of the many festivals and ancient religious traditions that were "Christianized" over time. For instance, the December 25 date we mark as Jesus's birth was taken either, depending on the source, from the ancient Druids who celebrated the Winter Solstice at that time or from the Roman festival of the Unconquered Sun. Either way, we really don't know the precise day Jesus was born—I guess there's a 1-in-365 chance it was December 25—but it doesn't really matter. It's not about a specific date as much as the incarnational event that commemorates the moment God took on human flesh.

Ditto Christmas trees. The Druids began the practice of bringing greenery into their homes to celebrate this same midwinter pagan festival to offer encouragement to the sun, their object of worship.

There are various examples of this adoption of ancient practices into the Christian tradition. I see no shame or dishonor in this, but rather new understandings of old traditions—the placing of "new wine into old wineskins." Or freshly brewed coffee into old mugs.

Coffee and Reformation

There's an old joke that says when Europeans began drinking coffee instead of alcohol, they started thinking straight and became Protestants. That's not entirely true since the timing doesn't exactly line up, but the Protestant Reformation did take off as coffee arrived on the continent, and alcohol was increasingly looked upon with suspicion by many Reformers.

While it's hard for us to imagine an entire society spending a significant portion of the day buzzed, it's true that beer in particular provided a significant percentage of the average person's daily caloric intake. It comprised an essential part of the medieval diet for both adults and children, partly for health reasons, as water was particularly unhygienic and was a major cause of disease in the Middle Ages. Beer or ale, rather than café au lait, functioned as the European morning drink of choice. When historians speak of the Dark Ages, they are not referring to black coffee.

The Reformation's emphasis on alcohol moderation wasn't entirely successful, but it did at least raise the issue in public consciousness. A quote attributed to Martin Luther blurs some of the lines: "Whoever drinks beer, he is quick to sleep; whoever sleeps long, does not sin; whoever does not sin, enters Heaven! Thus, let us drink beer!" Yet, he also railed against "demon alcohol."

Either way, with boiled water integral to its preparation, coffee consumption was deemed safe. And, whether coincidental or not, once coffee arrived, Reformation and then Enlightenment ideas swept the continent. Who knows? Perhaps people did simply need to wake up.

Cappuccino Legend

Another great coffee legend with religious connotations revolves around the origin of the word *cappuccino*. In 1520, Franciscan monk Matteo da Bascio fretted that his order had strayed too far from Francis's original vision, so he broke away and founded the Capuchin order, basing it on poverty, simplicity, and austerity. Persecuted by the religious authorities for their unwelcome innovations, Friar Matteo and his companions were forced into hiding. Offered sanctuary by Camaldolese monks, they took on the coffee-colored hood (cappuccio) of the Camaldolese order as a sign of gratitude.

When what became known as cappuccino was introduced in Italy, it allegedly acquired the name because the drink closely resembled Capuchin monks with their shaved heads and brown hooded cowls. In Italian, *cappuccino* means "little cap," a good description of the foamed milk that forms the head on top of the espresso base. When I toured the ancient catacombs beneath Rome, our tour guide offered yet another possibility—that the Capuchin monks themselves loved coffee but, in the days of Christian coffee controversy, they felt compelled to hide their coffee under the cap of foam. In the next breath, she admitted this was absurd.

An offshoot of this story claims a Capuchin friar named Marco d'Aviano invented the drink.[2] When a large Ottoman Turkish army marched on Vienna in 1683, Pope Innocent XI sent d'Aviano to rally and unite the outnumbered Christian soldiers. After the monk led them in prayer, the troops went on to victory.

The fleeing Turks left behind sacks of coffee, which the Christians found too bitter for their liking, so the friar sweetened the drink with milk and honey. Whatever the truth, Pope John Paul II beatified Marco d'Aviano in 2003, presumably for having done miracles other than allegedly inventing cappuccino.

Patron Saint of Coffee

As you might imagine, there is indeed a patron saint of coffee. As you might *not* imagine, a cup of coffee never once passed his lips.

Saint Drogo of Sebourg (1105–1186) was a Frenchman born into a family of means in Épinoy, in the extreme northern part of the country. However, his father died before he was born, and his mother died in childbirth, leaving him an orphan. Perhaps feeling immense guilt over his entrance into the world, Drogo found himself drawn to an ascetic lifestyle and forsook all worldly wealth. He earned his living as a shepherd, working dutifully for a pious woman in the town of Sebourg, near the Belgian border, and he undertook numerous religious pilgrimages to Rome.

Known for his gentle piety and kindness to all he encountered, Drogo became renowned for his ability to bi-locate—appearing in two places at once. Numerous witnesses claimed they saw him attending mass and working out in the fields *at the same time*.

As a young man, an unnamed bodily affliction struck Drogo, which left him deformed and ended his ability to go on pilgrimages. The townspeople helped Drogo build a cell attached to the local church that included a small window so he could participate in the liturgies. Which doesn't sound creepy at all. Drogo spent the next four decades living in solitude and subsisting on water, barley, and communion while praying and offering counsel to anyone who stopped by to visit.

Why is Drogo the patron saint of coffee and coffeehouses? My theory is his ability to bi-locate mimicked the effects of an over-caffeinated multitasker. But I really have no idea.

Coffee Cantata

Johann Sebastian Bach (1685–1750) stands out as one of history's most prolific and popular composers of sacred music. His cantatas, organ preludes, hymn tunes, and mass settings include some of the most uplifting and inspirational music ever written. From his *St. Matthew's Passion* to the *B Minor Mass* to "Jesu, Joy of Man's Desiring," Bach has greatly enriched the devotional life of Christians for generations.

What you may not know is that this avowed coffee drinker also wrote what is popularly known as the Coffee Cantata. It's actually a one-act comic opera he composed in about 1735 that revolves around a coffee-loving young woman named Aria. Her mean-spirited and clearly uncaffeinated father tries to prevent her from enjoying the energy-inducing drink. Which leads Aria to such wonderfully bitter complaint:

> Father sir, but do not be so harsh!
> If I couldn't, three times a day,
> be allowed to drink my little cup of coffee,
> in my anguish I will turn into
> a shriveled-up roast goat.
>
> Ah! How sweet coffee tastes,
> more delicious than a thousand kisses,
> milder than muscatel wine.

Coffee, I have to have coffee,
and, if someone wants to pamper me,
ah, then bring me coffee as a gift![3]

Fortunately for everyone involved, father and daughter reconcile by the end, and Aria receives a marriage contract signed by her father that guarantees her three cups of coffee per day.

The historical context of Bach's Coffee Cantata does point to the drink's continued controversy into the eighteenth century. The Prussian ruler Frederick the Great (1712–1786) succeeded militarily and economically throughout his long reign, but one less-than-productive endeavor was his attempt to limit spending on coffee. Concerned that his people spent too much money on coffee, he sought to have its use limited to the upper classes by taxing it as a luxury item. He also became convinced that coffee would hurt the monetary success of local and government-owned breweries. Frederick thus forbade local roasting of coffee and unleashed a brigade of coffee sniffers to snoop around German towns and expose anyone caught roasting coffee, which, as we know, has a distinct (and wonderful) aroma.

In 1777, Frederick went so far as to publish a pro-beer, anti-coffee manifesto:

It is disgusting to notice the increase in the quantity of coffee used by my subjects, and the amount of money that goes out of the country in consequence. Everybody is using coffee. If possible, this must be prevented. My people must drink beer. His Majesty was brought up on beer, and so were his ancestors, and his officers. Many battles have been fought and won by soldiers nourished on beer; and the King does not believe that coffee-drinking soldiers can be depended upon to endure hardship or to beat his enemies in case of the occurrence of another war.[4]

In the end, Frederick realized limiting coffee was quixotic at best and, instead, created a royal monopoly on coffee roasting, thus ending the stigma while simultaneously enriching the royal coffers.

Italy and the Rise of Espresso

When espresso first entered the consciousness of the average American, linguistic confusion was legion. Nothing says I'm-an-American-who-doesn't-care-about-your-culture quite like ordering an "expresso." There's no such thing. Even "Weird Al" Yankovic, the crazy-haired, iconic comedic songwriter, mentioned the issue in his clever and amusing "Word Crimes" song, which has over forty million views on YouTube. "No X in espresso!" he sings.

For espresso lovers, it is coffee in its purest form. I'm not a huge espresso guy, preferring drip coffee, but a shot of espresso being expertly pulled from a sleek and mysterious machine in a trendy coffee bar just oozes romance. For me, it evokes zipping past the Roman Coliseum on a Vespa while chain-smoking unfiltered Italian cigarettes with one hand and sipping a double shot of espresso with the other.

A rather modern innovation in the grand scheme of coffee history, espresso is linked to the Industrial Revolution. Nineteenth-century coffeehouses had become immensely popular, but the process for making coffee was rather slow. That's fine if you prefer to linger over your coffee and, say, plan a revolution, but if you have somewhere to be, you may crave something a bit more efficient.

Enter the Italian inventors who used steam technology to speed up the coffee-making process. Angelo Moriondo of Turin, Italy (there is no corresponding Shroud of Espresso), was granted the first patent for such a machine in 1884, though his apparatus appears to have been a one-off. In the early twentieth century, an inventor from Milan named Luigi Bezzera took Moriondo's concept and improved upon it by introducing the portafilter and multiple brewheads. Instead of waiting five minutes for your coffee, it was brewed in a matter of seconds! Unfortunately, Bezzera's machine also used an open flame, which, aside from being as dangerous as it sounds, led to inconsistency in flavor. Also, Bezzera ran out of money.

Luckily, another Italian inventor, Desiderio Pavoni, bought Bezzera's patents in 1903 and continued to improve upon the design. His innovations included the steam wand and the pressure-release valve, the latter meaning baristas no longer risked hot coffee being splashed all over their faces. The machine, named the Ideale, was introduced at the 1906 Milan Fair, and Pavoni dubbed the resulting coffee drink *caffè espresso*. A master marketer, Pavoni's machines and the revolutionary drink caught on quickly. Soon enough, as Italian workers lined up for a quick shot of caffeine, the term espresso entered everyday vocabulary.[5]

Espresso is still coffee, by the way. It's not a type of bean or roast, which often confuses people. The method of preparation, specifically the way pressurized hot water is forced over the grounds to create a concentrated and robust coffee drink, sets it apart. There's a popular misconception that Pavoni's term referred to the speed at which the coffee was produced—as in the English word "express." Nope. In Italian, *espresso* means "to force out," thus denoting the brewing method. Once again, Weird Al wins the day.

A barista produces a modern espresso shot by placing finely ground and densely packed coffee into a portafilter, the implement used to hold the ground beans. After tamping the grounds down into a cake-like layer, the preparer places the portafilter into the machine and directs hot water through the grounds to create the beloved drink.

While filtered coffee uses gravity to extract water through the grounds, espresso machines use pressurized water, leading to quick brewing and the rich taste that is the hallmark of a perfectly pulled shot of espresso. You can geek out on the physics, if that's your thing: as espresso machines use water pressure up to 130 pounds per square inch (PSI). In scientific terms, that's nine bars of pressure, or the equivalent of nine times the atmospheric pressure at sea level, so you'd have to dive about 300 feet into the ocean to create the same amount of pressure used to make the ideal espresso.

Espresso is typically served in tiny china cups, often called a demitasse (meaning *half cup* in French). I like taking close-ups of my hand holding an espresso cup and posting them on Instagram because this makes my hand look *huge*. Like I'm André the Giant or Gulliver. Espresso also serves as the base for a host of popular drinks like cappuccinos, lattes, Americanos, mochas, and macchiatos, none of which get served in the small espresso cups. Which means if you want to appear oversized on social media, you'll have to take pictures with your niece's dollhouse furniture.

For years, espresso intimidated me. It seemed bitter and more like a caffeine medicine—something to suck down but not enjoy.

Espresso aficionados tell me this is often the case for people who try espresso in less than ideal conditions. Like your friend's $200 kitchen-counter espresso machine that looks impressive but can't produce anything approaching the optimal espresso. Even in many outstanding restaurants, you may spot a fancy machine, but if no one on staff has been properly trained in the fine art of making espresso, it will disappoint.

Espresso should taste rich and sweet and be topped with a delightful, velvety foam known as crema. I finally figured this out, but not until that same trip to Rome where I tracked down Clement VIII. Over four days in the Eternal City, I exclusively drank espresso (well, some red wine too, if I'm honest). I'm not sure how Romulus, Julius Caesar, or Herod the Great functioned in Rome without espresso, but no one these days seems to do so. Espresso, like the Roman Coliseum and linguini, feels omnipresent. Beyond the espresso bars and restaurants, nearly every boutique shop and plenty of lower-end ones have sleek espresso machines on the premises—just in case. I even had a double shot of the stuff at Caffè Vaticano, located just outside the walls of the Vatican, before touring the Sistine Chapel. *Habemus espresso* is not an expression used by the Swiss Guard.

My favorite espresso, however, came from an iconic little place around the corner from the Pantheon called Sant' Eustachio il Caffè. In many ways, it's a typical Italian espresso bar, packed with regulars drinking shots standing at the bar and tourists ordering fancy coffee drinks while lingering at the outdoor tables. The bow-tied baristas ply their craft with graceful, no-nonsense efficiency (no frivolous latte art on Bryna's cappuccino!), and I needed a spoon to scoop out the remains of the world-renowned crema.

It didn't hurt that the café, founded in 1938, was named for a second-century Roman saint. A poster of Saint Eustachio (or Eustace), a revered soldier-saint commemorated on the Roman Catholic, Anglican, and Orthodox calendars, hung on the wall of the cozy coffee shop. According to tradition, Eustachio, originally

Drinking my favorite espresso in Rome at Sant' Eustachio il Caffè.

known by his given name Placidus, served as a general under the Roman emperor Trajan. While hunting one day outside Rome, he looked up and saw a vision of a crucifix between a stag's antlers. Some might dream of a venison dinner, but Placidus immediately converted to Christianity and changed his name to Eustachio, meaning *steadfast* in Greek.

The café's logo incorporates an antlered deer with a cross atop its head. If this sounds vaguely familiar, a similar design is used for the German alcoholic beverage Jägermeister (literally, "Hunter-Master"), though they claim the *other* saint who spied a crucifix rising out of a stag's head, Saint Hubertus. You'll be glad to know there's a cocktail called the Javameister that incorporates Jägermeister and black coffee, topped with whipped cream. But that's a subject for a different book.

Fortunately, there are cheaper ways to develop a taste for espresso than traveling to Rome. Sometimes Little Italy or your favorite coffee shop will just have to do. Although nothing quite beats the romance of drinking espresso in the country where it all began.

God's House, Not Maxwell's House: Coffee and Judaism

One cannot attain presence of mind without the aid of coffee.

—Hezekiah da Silva, seventeenth-century Italian rabbi

It's a bad joke. A sexist joke. The kind of joke told around the campfire by the really dorky middle-aged camp chaplain. It seems a husband and wife were arguing about who should make coffee in the morning. The wife says, "Since you're up before me, you should do it." The husband disagrees saying, "It's part of the cooking, so it's your responsibility." "No," the wife says, "it's in the Bible that the man makes coffee." The husband says, "Prove it." The wife opens the family Bible and sure enough, there it is: He-brews.

Coffee in Judaism

Parallel discussions of religious law among faith communities serve as a hallmark of the coffee-faith connection. For Muslims, the issue revolved around the definition of *intoxicant* in the Qur'an. For sixteenth- and seventeenth-century Jews, the question involved whether or not this new drink was kosher—that is, consistent with and legal under the Law of Moses and therefore fit for consumption.

A number of *Halachic* (the collective body of Jewish laws) questions surrounding the consumption of coffee arose. The first considered the question of *Bishul Akum*, the prohibition against certain foods prepared by a non-Jew (*goy*). Resolution revolved around the argument that, at its essence, coffee is merely flavored water. During the harvesting, roasting, and brewing process, coffee beans only come into contact with water. Thus coffee fell under the *Halachic* status of water under the *Bishul Akum*, a legal exemption, as water may be consumed without cooking.

So coffee was consumable by the average Jew, regardless of who prepared it. However, as the *Talmud*, the collection of ancient writings based on oral and written Jewish law, does proclaim that an *Adam Cha'shuv*, or prominent person, should avoid drinking water cooked by a *goy*, some observant Jews nevertheless refrain from this practice.

The problem came later when additives, flavorings, and the process of decaffeination became part of coffee drinking. Most equipment used to process and roast coffee is not used for any other purpose, so coffee beans themselves are considered kosher and no special certification is necessary.

Typically, flavors (hazelnut, vanilla, chocolate, etc.) added after the roasting process via flavor extract are considered *Pareve* (prepared without dairy or meat and therefore permissible). However, all flavored coffees require a kosher certification, requiring two necessary steps. First, the material, in this case the coffee bean, as well as the processing machinery or utensils involved must be permissible under Jewish law. Second, a rabbi must observe and certify the production process.

In other words, it's complicated. So much so that there's even a popular website, www.kosherstarbucks.com, that helps observant Jews navigate the world's most popular coffee shop.

The process of decaffeinating coffee posed other issues. Generally, decaf is made by soaking beans in a solvent that removes the caffeine prior to roasting. A number of different chemicals are involved, but one of the common ones is ethyl acetate, a grain-based solvent and thus considered *Chometz* (food mixed with leaven and therefore not kosher). Other decaffeinating methods exist, including the Swiss Water Process, but rabbis recommend only drinking kosher-certified decaffeinated coffee.

The other parallel between early Muslim and Jewish use, once legality was established, involved the use of coffee as fuel for night prayers. The stimulating effects of coffee immediately became a boon to the spiritual life of the faithful, as we saw with the midnight rite known as the *Tikkun Chatzot* for Jews and the night prayers of Sufi mystics.

After settling the debate over whether coffee was kosher, the rabbis had to determine which prayer would be said over coffee. After some back and forth, it was generally accepted that the generic prayer over food, or *Shehakol*, would suffice: "Blessed are You, Hashem, our God, King of the universe, through Whose word everything came to be."

The next question for the Jewish community after the introduction of the coffeehouse revolved around whether observant Jews could, in good faith, drink coffee at shops owned by non-Jews. In the early days of coffee culture, before home brewing became normative, coffee drinkers sought out public stalls or shops to purchase their coffee. We have a record of one mid-sixteenth-century Cairo rabbi, David ibn Abi Zimra—he ruled that Jews could drink coffee prepared by *Goyim*, but he counseled them against patronizing coffeehouses, suggesting they have their coffee delivered to their homes.[1]

Nonetheless, in 1632 members of the Jewish community in the Italian port city of Livorno imported the first coffee into Italy before opening the country's first coffeehouses and sending large shipments of coffee beans to Venice. With rabbinic support, the Jewish community as a whole did embrace coffee. It's said that the seventeenth-century Italian rabbi Hezekiah da Silva once declared, "One cannot attain presence of mind without the aid of coffee."[2] No argument here.

With their international trade connections, it's not surprising that Jews played an instrumental role in the early years of the coffee trade. Granted, discrimination played a role in this as trading opened as an avenue only because Jews typically found themselves barred from participation in agriculture and craft guilds.

Anti-Semitism also reared its ugly head in local governments throughout the early days of coffee's European foray. Jews had permission to trade in coffee because the ruling class did not consider it an important or economically lucrative commodity. When the coffee boom fully arrived, many municipalities passed legislation forbidding Jews to compete with Christian merchants. Rabbi Elliot Schoenberg cites one example in Frankfurt, Germany, where from the 1760s through the 1780s, city officials enacted laws denying Jews the right to sell coffee.[3]

One of the best-known historical Jewish coffee connections comes through a man known to history only as Jacob the Jew. A Lebanese entrepreneur, Jacob opened the first coffeehouse in Oxford, England, in 1850. The oft-cited source for this is Antony Wood's 1691 book titled *Athenae Oxonienses* in which he writes: "Jacob, a Jew, opened a Coffee house at the Angel, in the Parish of St Peter in the East, Oxon, and there it was by some, who delighted in the novelty, drank."[4] So, the first coffeehouse in the English-speaking world offered a drink popularized by Muslims, was owned by a Jew, and operated out of the Angel Inn. A holy trifecta!

In his book *A Rich Brew: How Cafés Created Modern Jewish Culture*, Shachar Pinsker writes about the impact of coffeehouses on Jewish identity. As Jews migrated throughout Europe and eventually to the United States, cafés served as sanctuaries for the intellectual and cultural experience that defined Jewish character. "Jews were often owners of cafés. Jewish writers have written in cafés, and they have written about cafés. Jewish intellectuals have used the café to create a place to argue with each other. Jewish merchants have made the café into a negotiating table. The café, in other words, has been an essential facet of the modern Jewish experience and has been critical to its complex mixture of history and fiction, reality and imagination, longing and belonging, consumption and sociability, idleness and productivity."[5]

In recent decades, another Jewish coffee entrepreneur has reinvented coffee culture. Perhaps you've heard of Howard Schultz, who acquired Starbucks in 1987 and opened a few coffee shops around the globe.

Good to the Last Drop

When people ask me why I'm passionate about serving good coffee in church, I often say, "Because it's God's house, not Maxwell's House." At least I used to until it was pointed out to me by my friend Meredith Gould that Maxwell House coffee is inextricably linked to the Passover Haggadah (the text that sets forth the order of the Seder meal). Curious as to what she meant, I researched this further.

Many Jewish immigrants arrived in the United States in the early twentieth century and brought with them their love of coffee from the Old Country. As they gathered to celebrate Passover with the traditional Seder dinner, which tells the story of Moses leading the Israelites out of bondage in Egypt, they encountered a legal challenge to drinking coffee during this most holy time. A misunderstanding arose, and many Jewish sellers started classifying coffee beans as legumes, which were prohibited during Passover.

As we've seen, coffee beans are not vegetables but fruit, the consumption of which is permitted. Enter coffee savior Joseph Jacobs, head of one of New York's first Jewish advertising agencies. In 1923 he had the brilliant marketing idea to certify Maxwell House coffee (which was made by the non-Jewish General Foods) as "Kosher for Passover" and ran ads to that effect.

Then in 1932 came the real coup: he convinced Maxwell House to print copies of the Passover Haggadah to be given away with cans of the company's coffee. These iconic Haggadahs contained advertisements for the coffee and became prevalent in Jewish households throughout America. Over the years, Maxwell House has distributed over fifty-five million of these booklets, still printing one million each year, and the Jacobs/Maxwell House partnership continues as the longest-running sales promotion in advertising history, one that has done much to connect Judaism to the coffee everyone knows by the slogan Good to the Last Drop.[6]

I actually held one of these Maxwell House Haggadahs in my hand as a child. My mother's family emigrated from Russia in the late nineteenth century as Jewish immigrants, complete with Ellis Island street cred. My mother converted to Christianity during college, but as a boy we joined her extended family for Passover services at the home of my Uncle Jules and Aunt Estelle in Morris Plains, New Jersey.

I mostly remember being allowed a few sips of sickeningly sweet Manischewitz wine (but never the coffee!) as the exodus story ritually unfolded amid the consumption of bitter herbs and matzoh ball soup. But I also recall the after-dinner coffee consumed by the adults, as my cousins and I raced around the house in search of the hidden matzoh and the accompanying cash prize of a crisp $2 bill.

I have no idea if my relatives bought into the marketing and drank Maxwell House after the Seder dinner. I somehow doubt it. Yet topping the family gathering off with coffee (Kosher for Passover!) enhanced the ritual action of the evening and added an exclamation point of warm comfort.

Coffee, Solomon, and the Queen of Sheba

While coffee wasn't officially discovered until the ninth century, coffee lore exists surrounding the famed Queen of Sheba, who appears in the Second Book of Chronicles (dated to about the sixth century BCE) well before any mention of coffee. She came to visit King Solomon in Jerusalem, arriving with a very great caravan of "camels bearing spices and very much gold and precious stones" (2 Chronicles 9:1). She was overwhelmed at Solomon's wisdom, his palace, and the God of Israel. As a token of her visit, she presented him with gold, spices, and jewels, and Solomon reciprocated with similar gifts.

Biblical scholars believe that Sheba equates to the kingdom of Saba in present-day Yemen, and that it also included parts of Ethiopia. Perhaps this connection to coffee's origins fuels the notion that coffee was among the gifts presented by the queen to Solomon.[7] Certainly no historic evidence exists, but we can add this to the numerous legends about this regal ruler that abound in Christianity, Judaism, and Islam.

Solomon appears in another coffee story as well. According to the Arab writer Abu al-Tayyib, in his travels the great king came to a place where the townspeople were afflicted with an unspecified disease. It seems the archangel Gabriel then appeared and directed

Solomon to roast some coffee beans, brew the drink, and serve it to the diseased sufferers. Naturally, the cures came instantly. Despite this miracle, apparently everyone forgot about coffee for the next thousand years.

Coffee Cake

To many folks, nothing goes better with coffee than . . . coffee cake. Although the original Jewish coffee cakes called for coffee as a main ingredient, today it's caffeine-free. Which is why I don't eat the stuff.

Tracing the history of coffee cake means heading back to central Europe, and in particular Germany. There, the combination of coffee, cake, and conversation became pervasive enough to garner its own name: *kaffeeklatsch*. The German women who baked and served this coffee-infused cake in tube-like pans that formed a hole in the middle referred to it as *Bundkuchen*.

Returning to America, we find ourselves in the midst of a midwestern Jewish community in the 1950s. The Minneapolis chapter of Hadassah, the Jewish women's volunteer organization founded in 1912, asked a designer named H. David Dalquist to help them construct a cake pan that would allow them to re-create the recipes brought over by their mothers when they emigrated to America. The resulting design became known as the Bundt pan, a standard of American kitchens for generations.[8]

Dalquist, the owner of the Nordic Ware company, originally planned to christen it the Bund pan. Some speculate he added the extra letter at the end to distance himself from the German American Bund, a pro-Nazi group established in 1936.

In contemporary Jewish homes, coffee cake remains a staple, often served for breakfast and on holidays. Though thanks to Drake's Cakes (which produced the first kosher cake on the market), you can have coffee cake whenever you fill up your car at the gas station.

Coffee in the Garden of Eden?

One of the seminal stories of Hebrew Scripture is the account of Adam and Eve in the garden of Eden, at the center of which stands the Tree of the Knowledge of Good and Evil. For generations, this story of original sin has revolved around an apple, yet Scripture never mentions an apple—the author of Genesis refers simply to a "fruit."

Some have even speculated whether it was actually the coffee tree standing at the heart of the creation story. If, as Antony Wild suggests in his book *Coffee: A Dark History*, coffee has long been associated with cognition and self-awareness, wouldn't the coffee tree have made a more engaging foil than, say, a Granny Smith?[9] I mean, suddenly realizing you're naked must be the ultimate moment of consciousness, and drinking coffee does bring clarity.

Those who have traveled to the Ethiopian Highlands have often remarked on its Eden-like landscape. The scenery and lush vegetation lend themselves to a certain biblical view, and the intersection between the place where both coffee and humanity were discovered proves irresistible to speculation. Genetically speaking, humankind's oldest known ancestors lived in the same area as coffee's initial discovery. Lucy, that darling of anthropology students everywhere, known scientifically as *Australopithecus*, was unearthed in Ethiopia.

The book of Enoch, an ancient book of noncanonical Scripture stumbled upon by the eighteenth-century explorer James Bruce in (where else?) Ethiopia, contains a description of the Tree of Knowledge that could well suggest the coffee tree. Enoch prophesies,

> It was like a species of the tamarind tree, bearing fruit which resembled grapes extremely fine; and its fragrance extended to a considerable distance. I exclaimed, how beautiful is this tree, and how delightful is its appearance! Then holy Raphael, an angel who was with me, answered and said, This is the tree of knowledge, of which thy ancient father and thy aged mother ate, who were before thee; and who, obtaining knowledge, their eyes being opened, and knowing themselves to be naked, were expelled from the garden. (Enoch 31:4–5)

Okay, I'm not insisting the famous tree was definitively a coffee tree. It's fun to speculate, though, right?

The Power of Ritual

Last comes the beverage of the Orient shore, Mocha, far off, the fragrant berries bore. Taste the dark fluid with a dainty lip, digestion waits on pleasure as you sip.

—Pope Leo XII (1760–1829)

From the beginning of time, patterns of ritual action have coexisted with the human condition. Ritual provides meaning and comfort and adds a layer of stability and control atop a chaotic and ever-changing world. From rites of initiation to religious puberty rites to prescribed ceremonies around death, we crave ritual.

Religious rituals are as ancient as humanity itself, and every community of faith has sacred rites, symbols, and actions. Yet ritual transcends the realm of faith and enters into nearly every aspect of our lives. When you're introduced to your wife's boss, you engage in one of the most common rituals in the Western world by shaking the person's hand. This accepted social norm removes the potential awkwardness of the situation. Conversely, if instead of shaking hands, you barked at the moon, that would change the dynamic of the expected social currency. It may also quickly lead to your becoming a single-income family.

The preparation and drinking of coffee stands as one of the world's most universal rituals. Methods may differ, but every coffee-drinking household has its sacred rituals. They're worth exploring, and I invite you to intentionally think about your own daily experience.

Earliest Coffee Rituals

We've seen the extent to which coffee meshed with Sufi prayer rituals, but there's increasing evidence that the ritual use of coffee predates even these early practices. The Oromo people, an ancient tribe linked to Ethiopia, still exist today in Ethiopia, northern Kenya, and Somalia. The most recent population estimates cite up to thirty-five million Oromo people, with religious leanings mostly split between Islam and the Ethiopian Orthodox Church. But a small percentage follow the traditional religion, Waaqeffannaa, whose adherents, known as Waaqeeffatoota, worship the creator god Waaqa.

Tracing Oromo history proves difficult, as much got passed down through oral tradition, but most believe they have lived in

Africa for at least one millennium, perhaps originally migrating from Asia. Regardless of their religious beliefs, many Oromo still practice the traditional coffee ceremonies handed down from their ancestors as a celebration of their common ethnicity.

In Oromo tradition, the coffee plant is imbued with divine properties based on the belief it first grew out of the tears of Waaqa. The coffee creation story developed around this conviction begins with a man who refused to do Waaqa's will. This led to both Waaqa's supreme disappointment and the man's death. When Waaqa visited the spot where the man had died and saw his corpse, tears burst forth from his eyes. At that very moment, a coffee tree sprouted from the place of Waaqa's tears.[1]

In Oromo tradition, the color green symbolizes fertility, thus, the ever-green coffee plant is perceived as a sign of Waaqa's blessing. Farmers plant coffee trees at the entrances to their farms—not to cultivate, in this case, but as a sign of Waaqa's presence.

The traditional Oromo coffee ceremony highlights two things: coffee and community. In the go-go society in which we live, where Keurig machines and fast-food joints are the norm, the Ethiopian coffee ritual preserved by the Oromo slows everything down. The woman of the house acts as high priest of the coffee ceremony, which, while an act of hospitality and service, flips the norms of patriarchal culture. From washing the beans to roasting them on an open flame to sharing the aroma with guests to grinding the roasted beans in a mortar and pestle to reverently placing the grounds into a clay pot to pouring water over them, each step is performed deliberately and with great intention. In between the prescribed steps, conversation fills the air as the communal spirit of life together is built up cup by cup.

During the ceremony, which lasts up to three hours, Oromo elders recite certain prayers at appointed times, such as: *Bunaa fi nagaa nuuf kenni* (Give us coffee and peace) and *Manaan fi ollaan nuuf toli* (Bless our home and our neighbors). The ceremony's hostess holds up the hot clay vessel and prays to Waaqa: *Gubaan siif baadha gubaa nu oolchi* (I am carrying hot for your glory, protect us from hot) and *Guutuu siif dhaabna guutuu nuuf godhi* (We rise full for you make us full).[2]

This type of ceremony may not fit into our daily routines, but it does remind us to at least slow down occasionally. The Oromo also help us recall that the whole history of coffee's origins, while murky, encompasses one of humankind's most unique and life-giving features: ritual.

Morning Ritual

Perhaps the one ritual that unites people all over the world is the preparation of their morning coffee. Different methods exist, of course, from the automatic drip maker to the French press to the Chemex to the vacuum pot. (The IV drip is not an approved method.) In each, the goal remains the same: extracting flavor from ground coffee beans by infusing them with water to create a beverage.

In American kitchens, this can take various forms. From the guy stumbling downstairs, taking his bag of Folgers out of the freezer, and hastily scooping out enough for the first pot of the day to the urban hipster grinding his single-origin beans, weighing them on a digital scale, heating water to just under boiling in his gooseneck kettle, and carefully pouring the water over the grounds.

For some, brewing is the ritual's key. For others, it's the procuring of the drink itself. This may be the professional woman stopping by Starbucks on her way to catch the commuter rail, the guy in the hard hat pulling into the Dunkin' Donuts drive-through to pick up a Box O' Joe for his work crew, or the laptop-toting freelancer setting up shop in his neighborhood coffeehouse.

Think about your own morning ritual. How did it start? Has it evolved over the years? Have you experimented with different brewing techniques?

For someone who loves coffee as much as I do, for years my own method was oddly hands off. In our house, Bryna made the morning coffee. Mostly, it's because she drinks it first thing. You know those T-shirts that read But First . . . Coffee? That's her motto. If I stood between Bryna and her morning coffee, things would not end well for me.

Like many people, we used an automatic drip machine for the majority of our life together. We've been through several over the years—they don't last forever, like your grandmother's stove-top percolator did. Yes, we grind our own beans; no, we don't keep them in the freezer. I think the machine has a timer but, like setting the VCR to record, we never figured out how it actually works.

Often my first cup of coffee is fine. Nothing special; more of a caffeine distribution system. For my good coffee, I tended to let the professionals handle things. In this regard, Bryna and I differ—and maybe this comes from being a relatively late adopter of coffee. I don't need it first thing in the morning. I generally eat my breakfast first, *before* coffee, which I realize many of you can't relate to. At all. Certainly, that's not how Bryna's relationship with coffee works.

In the end, whether prepared hastily or reverently, coffee reaches our cup via ritual. And ritual, in developing patterns of intimacy, is a form of prayer by any other name.

Prayerful Preparation

The prayerful preparation of coffee can serve as an anchor for the rest of the day, at least on occasion. Like if you're the first person up in the morning and the kitchen is unusually calm and quiet. Or it's the weekend and no one's rushing out the door to work and school.

From my own tradition, I like to look back to the approach of Saint Benedict of Nursia, the fourth-century monk and father of Western monasticism. From Benedict, we learn of the connection between body, mind, and spirit. He also teaches the importance of seeing the sacred in everyday, mundane things. For instance, when a monk under Benedict's rule was engaged in manual labor, he was encouraged to view the rake or shovel as a holy object. As long as the work was offered to the glory of God, the implement in his hands was viewed as worthy and as sacred an object as a communion chalice. Approaching life from this perspective can change your entire outlook and infuse deeper meaning in all things.

Applying this concept to making coffee allows us to turn our ritual preparation into a form of morning devotions. We can prayerfully grind our beans, mindful of the many hands and lives of those who brought them into our midst. We can give thanks for the water of baptism as we slowly pour the water into the coffee maker or offer a prayer to the sustainer of all creation, whose rain waters the earth, giving life and growth. We can take in the coffee's aroma, pausing for a rare moment of reflection.

Yes, there are times when we're just trying to make it through the day. But on those days in between, I encourage you to slow down, whatever your brewing method, and revel in the experience and joyful gift of this beautiful beverage.

Upping My Coffee Game

Writing and researching a book about coffee has led to some coffee experimentation on my part. While I usually let the trained baristas handle my specialty coffee fix, I decided I needed to walk the coffee walk if I wanted to talk the coffee talk. Plus, I realized if I continued to buy good coffee beans for home use, I owed it to the beans (and the farmers) to brew them in the best way possible. As Ruth Brown puts it in her snarky little book *Coffee Nerd*, "If you buy a really expensive hunk of beef, you don't cook it well-done; you cook it rare or medium-rare so you can still taste all the flavors and juices and things that *make* it an expensive piece of meat."[3] She was referring to not over-roasting beans, though the concept also holds true for the rest of the coffee-preparation process.

Most people ignore the fact that coffee is an agricultural product. We know this intellectually, but we tend to treat it as a commodity with an indefinite shelf life. Like an Easter Peep. Once freshly roasted coffee beans come into contact with oxygen, they immediately begin to degrade. Specialty coffee comes in vacuum-sealed bags for a reason—to keep the air out and the flavor in. True coffee lovers won't purchase pre-ground coffee because it'll be stale by the time it's brewed.

Most roasters post a "roasted on" date on their retail bags of coffee. If not, well, there's a reason for this and such operations should be avoided, no matter how eye-catching the packaging. While no single industry standard exists, most roasters concerned with quality control will pull beans off the shelves if they don't sell within two to four weeks. As with all things coffee-related, this is a matter of taste, but I've found that once you get used to fresh coffee, nothing else is palatable.

Anyway, I recently decided to heed this advice and intentionally transform my morning coffee ritual. Bryna thinks I'm a fool. ("*How much* are you spending on coffee equipment?" "*How long* is this going to take exactly?" "You better not get in my way in the morning!")

After conducting some research and talking to Bob at Redeye Roasters, I invested in a burr grinder, eight-cup Chemex, digital kitchen scale, and a gooseneck hot-water kettle. The first purchase was the grinder because, when talking to coffee geeks, that's the first thing they mention. And by mention, I mean look at you skeptically and say, "I assume you have a burr grinder." The first commandment of home brewing states that all grinders are not created equal.

A burr grinder (think pepper mill) grinds beans uniformly, as opposed to a blade grinder, which chops them like a ninja. That's not what you're looking for. You can tell whether it's a blade grinder by looking inside. If you see what looks like a mini propeller, you've encountered a blade grinder. Using such a grinder is obviously better than not using a grinder at all, but coffee aficionados recoil at the mere mention of blade grinders, partly because they insist on a uniform grind for consistent extraction and partly because the heat thrown off by blade grinders burns the beans. Mostly, though, they view using such grinders as the equivalent of sending their precious beans to the guillotine.

You can purchase either electric burr grinders or manual ones. Since I'm not a pioneer, I went with the electric version. You can get a decent one for home use for well under $100. Once it arrived, the question became what to do with our old, faithful blade grinder? Naturally, it's now in my office at church, which is where most things go that Bryna doesn't want around the house.

Next came the Chemex. As much as we love sleek and modern in all things—iPhones, high-end espresso machines, Lamborghinis— the Chemex is an elegant throwback. Designed in 1941 by German inventor Peter Schlumbohm, this retro glass pour-over coffeemaker displays beauty in its simplicity and design. You can visit the iconic hourglass-shaped body with conical neck, heatproof wooden collar, and leather strap in the permanent collection at the Museum of Modern Art in New York.

The Chemex also oozes cool, since James Bond used one in Ian Fleming's 1957 novel *From Russia with Love*. "Breakfast was Bond's favourite meal of the day. When he was stationed in London it was always the same. It consisted of very strong coffee, from De Bry in New Oxford Street, brewed in an American Chemex, of which he drank two large cups, black and without sugar."[4]

Beyond the look and style, a Chemex brews an incredibly clean cup of coffee, at least once you get the hang of it. The first step, after procuring superior-quality beans, is measuring out the perfect amount. Enter the digital scale. I picked up a Hario, but a variety of options exist. You just want one that measures in grams, includes a timer to ensure the proper extraction interval, and has a tare function, which allows you to zero-out the measurement. Why measure your beans precisely? Consistency. Pour-over coffee is all about the ratios, measured in grams, between ground coffee and water.

Besides the thick paper Chemex filters, the last thing a freshly minted coffee freak needs is an electric gooseneck kettle. Precision counts when doing a pour-over. Plenty of videos exist online to demonstrate the proper technique, but in the end, it just takes practice and about four minutes.

Bryna is now a Chemex convert and things have flipped around in the morning to where I've basically become her own personal barista. Alas. It's not much of a cross to bear for great coffee.

Cupping Coffee

Some ritual is more elaborate than others. While most baseball players have certain routines before stepping into the batter's box, like tapping the plate three times or taking two practices swings, Mike Hargrove stood out. Over his twelve-year career spanning the 1970s and '80s, mostly with the Cleveland Indians, Hargrove earned the nickname The Human Rain Delay for his deliberate actions before each pitch.

Driving both opposing pitchers and most fans nuts with his machinations, Hargrove would, among other things, adjust his batting gloves, hitch up his pants, adjust his helmet, knock the dirt out of his cleats, pull on his jersey, and adjust his gloves again. It was mesmerizing, if maddening, to watch.

In the coffee world, there's ritual coffee preparation and then there's cupping. People in the specialty coffee world don't *taste* different coffees, they *cup* them. Attending a pull-out-the-stops cupping with coffee professionals blows the mind. It's what synchronized swimming is to jumping into the pool to play Marco Polo with your kids. Rules, both written and unwritten, abound, along with strict etiquette and lots and lots of loud slurping.

Cupping with Mike Love at J. Hill Mill in Santa Ana, El Salvador.

While I've participated in several cuppings, and have enjoyed them, compared to the pros, I'm a rank amateur. It's great to taste different coffees from around the world in a single setting and soak in the ambience of high-end coffee culture, but the real intent of cupping is to create a consistent methodology for evaluating a coffee's quality before setting the price. Think wine connoisseurs sipping and spitting fine cabernets and pinot noirs using strict tasting protocols to assess quality, and you'll get the concept.

As with most rituals, a whole vocabulary exists that goes with cupping. Cuppers talk about fragrance, aroma, body, acidity, mouth feel, balance, and aftertaste, and that's before you even get into the flavors, or notes, themselves. The ultimate objective for professional cuppers is to score each coffee with grades ranging from 40 (below grade, disgusting) to 100 (super premium specialty, will change your life). Any score above 80 is considered specialty coffee. Participants use a uniform cupping sheet produced by the Specialty Coffee Association of America for grading, which they mark throughout the process. When Jesus said, "Do not judge, so that you may not be judged" (Matthew 7:1), he was not referring to cupping coffee.

Strict protocols of ritual rule the cupping process. The host, acting as high priest of the cupping table, lays out the freshly roasted and ground beans in small cups. Participants first smell the dry coffee to assess its fragrance. Next, hot water is poured into the cup of dry grounds and allowed to steep for three to four minutes, allowing the fullness of the coffee's flavor to emerge. A special silver cupping spoon, similar to a soup spoon, then breaks the crust that has formed over the cup and the cupper places his or her nose as close to the coffee as possible. Slowly stirring the coffee, the cupper inhales deeply and records a score. At this point, the coffee grounds that have floated to the top are removed and the coffee cools for up to twelve minutes (the true flavor of a coffee comes out as it cools). This is also the point at which I wipe coffee off my nose because, in my eagerness, I get too close to the cup.

Finally, it's time to taste (that is, slurp) the coffee and record the final score. Wander into a coffee cupping and it sounds like you've entered a bad table manners convention. The Queen of England would be mortified, but the idea is to aspirate the coffee over your tongue to bring out the fullness of the flavor. The astonishing sucking sounds remain the most memorable and loudest aspect of the cupping ritual.

In Central America, I had the chance to cup coffees in both Nicaragua and El Salvador. For roasters or coffee importers who travel to coffee farms around the world, assessing a variety of coffees from a particular region is an essential aspect of the trip. In Nicaragua, we cupped twenty-eight different coffees in one sitting. For me, it was enjoyable, albeit completely overwhelming and by the end they all tasted like coffee!

Watching Mike Love cup coffee is a thing of beauty. In addition to regularly cupping coffees from all over the world to make decisions on what to serve his customers, Mike often judges international coffee competitions. He's quick and efficient as he goes through the cups, pausing briefly over ones that are particularly flavorful or unusual, making mental notes about which ones to return to before assigning his final scores.

An eerie quiet falls over a cupping room as the experts make their evaluations. The only sounds being the quick bursts of high-pitched slurps as the cuppers taste the coffees and then spit them into plastic cups. Cuppers consider it bad form to share first impressions with others in the room for fear of influencing opinions through the power of suggestion, and even facial expressions are discouraged.

My own slurping technique is pretty weak, and I'm always grateful when a full cupping room masks my ineptitude. Everyone tells me it just takes practice, so I think I'll start slurping and spitting my morning coffee, which I'm sure Bryna wouldn't mind me doing as she eats breakfast and gets ready for work.

The good news with cupping, at least for amateurs, is that no wrong answers exist when it comes to personal taste. The more you do it, the more refined your palette becomes, and soon you can learn to distinguish, if nothing else, *why* you like certain coffees better than others. I'm always eager to go to cuppings and ask lots of questions. I may never be able to distinguish between those notes of mango and apricot, but at least I can now tell the difference between a coffee that tastes fruity as opposed to nutty. It's a start and an enjoyable ongoing journey of flavor discovery.

World Barista Championship

I'm not sure whether verbal analogies still play a role in college entrance exams, but I much preferred this type of SAT question to anything having to do with solving for X. In this vein, Cupping : Sipping :: World Barista Championship : Brewing.

I got a brief taste of this barista Super Bowl when I attended the World of Coffee expo in Amsterdam. This annual event resembles a kid-in-the-candy-shop experience for coffee enthusiasts and a command performance for coffee professionals. Bryna played the good sport as I dragged her through displays of shiny espresso machines, impressive roasters, high-tech grinders, and innovations such as an exercise bike that doubled as a coffee maker. Between the roaster village, brew bar, espresso bar, and cupping rooms, we were well-caffeinated as we tasted some of the world's best coffees. Unfortunately, the sport jackets made out of recycled burlap coffee sacks didn't come in my size. Yes, I tried them on.

The highlight, however, was witnessing a bit of the World Barista Championships (WBC). The fifty-five competing baristas, who qualified for the WBC by winning their national competitions, have fifteen minutes to prepare twelve beverages—four espresso drinks, four milk-based beverages, and four signature drinks. They're judged on presentation, style, technical skill, and creativity. As someone who must focus all his attention just to brew a decent cup of coffee, I watched with my jaw on the floor as these individuals dazzled the crowd. Granted, the only ones they really had to wow were the four judges, but with the entire world watching via livestream (or at least their friends and coworkers), the pressure was on.

While I didn't see her compete live, I was thrilled to learn that a young woman from Poland named Agnieszka "Aga" Rojewska took the crown. After years of male dominance, which reflects some darker realities of the coffee industry, Aga broke through the coffee glass ceiling and will hopefully inspire a whole new generation of women entering the field.

Witnessing the competition made me appreciate all the more my own local baristas—the ones I know by name, who start preparing my "usual" the moment I enter the coffee shop. Theirs is a vocation we too often take for granted—perhaps because we're not always fully awake yet. While I can take time to reflect upon being more appreciative, I should really just start leaving bigger tips.

Ancient Rituals Continue in Modern Times

We began this exploration of ritual with the ancient Oromo people. These early connections to the birthplace of coffee remain deeply embedded in the lives of those who live in the forests of Ethiopia. Deep in the heart of Kaffa, the Ethiopian region where coffee originated, coffee remains intertwined with spiritual practices. In his book *Where the Wild Coffee Grows*, Jeff Koehler writes of the continuing connection between forest, coffee, and spirit. There remain three sacrifices made throughout the year that mirror the life cycle of the revered coffee tree.[5]

When the tree flowers, a white animal is sacrificed—whether of feathers or fur is not important—that reflects the white blooms of the coffee tree. A few weeks later when the green buds first appear, a second sacrifice is offered using a dark animal. Finally, when the cherries ripen and turn dark red, a crimson or dark orange animal is sacrificed. The first two sacrifices are made in thanksgiving for coffee's arrival and as a hedge against disease or unseasonable weather. The third is made in thanksgiving for the fruitful crop.

I'm not about to tell our friends at PETA this news, but it does demonstrate the profound spiritual connection and ritual action that remains at coffee's ground zero. Popping the disposable K-cup into your Keurig machine somehow seems both quaint and insufficient in comparison.

8

Coming to America

Nobody can soldier without coffee.
—Ebenezer Nelson Gilpin, Union cavalryman,
in his diary, April 1865

While I hate to disappoint you, there is absolutely *no evidence* that coffee first came over to the New World on the *Mayflower*.

I personally can't imagine settling a new continent without the aid of coffee, but apparently the Pilgrims did just that. This is likely why things didn't always go so well for them and contributed to their obsession with that underwhelming rock in Plymouth (have you ever seen it? *Lame*).

Coffee probably first made it to the New World during the Dutch occupation of New York (New Amsterdam) in the mid-seventeenth century. The first reference to coffee in America occurred in 1668, as the Dutch West India Company had started trading in the commodity by then.[1] Sure, tea was the dominant drink, especially as the English settled New England and the mid-Atlantic states, but coffee had infiltrated our shores, and the American love affair with the beautiful bean would unfold soon enough.

I don't know when the first Schenck drank coffee in the New World, but my ancestors arrived in Brooklyn from Holland in the 1650s. In the Brooklyn Museum you can visit the 1675 Jan Martense Schenck House. I really need to return to see if there's a coffee vessel among the dark wood paneling and Delft ceramics.

Coffee initially appeared in an official record in New England in 1670. Dorothy Jones of Boston was granted a license to sell coffee and thereby became the first coffee trader in North America. I remain perplexed as to why she hasn't been added to the church's calendar of saints or at least given more acclaim. This is a big deal! To the point that if I had a daughter, she would definitely be named Dorothy Jones Schenck.[2]

We're not exactly sure why a woman was granted the first coffee license, but one can surmise that such work (brewing and serving coffee) was seen as beneath the dignity of the upstanding male adherents of the Protestant work ethic.

A Revolutionary Drink

While the rise of the famous European coffeehouse culture didn't exactly run a parallel course in America, one Boston coffeehouse was born whose reputation still reverberates. The Green Dragon Inn, Tavern, and Coffeehouse opened on Union Street in Boston in 1697 and played an integral role in the forming of the new republic. "Participants in New England's dynamic and colorful history occupied tables and sipped its coffee: redcoats, governors of the colonies, officers of the crown in powdered wigs, nobility, revolutionaries, conspirators, patriots, and generals of the Revolution."[3]

A number of coffeehouses dotted Boston at the time, many of which became known for and frequented by patrons of a particular political bent. Some of the names are wonderful: The King's Head, The India Queen, The British (which was wisely rebranded The American after the Revolution), The Bunch of Grapes, and The Royal Exchange. But it's The Green Dragon that lives on in revolutionary infamy.

Indeed, Daniel Webster called The Green Dragon the "headquarters of the Revolution," and it was on this very coffee-soaked hallowed ground that the Sons of Liberty formed and the Boston Tea Party was planned in response to the heavy taxation on tea imposed by the Stamp Act.[4]

I love that this iconic act of revolution was conceived in a coffeehouse. There's just something poetic about the idea of sipping coffee while plotting to dump tea into the Boston Harbor to protest taxes imposed by the British monarchy. I'd always assumed it was planned by a bunch of patriots drinking beer brewed by Sam Adams.

Far from a merely symbolic act, this rebellious event in 1773 had a direct impact on coffee drinking in America. Suddenly tea, the beloved drink of Loyalists and Revolutionaries alike, became anathema to those partial to the cause of American liberty, a tangible symbol of British royal oppression. Drinking tea was deemed unpatriotic, with coffee taking its place as the caffeinated pick-me-up of choice.

In a letter to his wife, John Adams wrote, "Tea must be universally renounced and I must be weaned, and the sooner the better."[5] Which was fine, but even (especially?) revolutionaries need their energy, so coffee became the patriotic drink of choice, a symbol of independence.

In Philadelphia, Merchants' Coffee House became the preferred hangout for members of the Continental Congress. It's believed that the first public reading of the Declaration of Independence took place at Merchants', amid the smell of freshly brewed coffee. The national fervor for coffee became so strong that the Continental Congress declared coffee the "national drink" following the events in Boston Harbor.

But in fairness, even before the protests over tea, these coffeehouses were gaining traction in the cities that forged the new nation. The London Coffeehouse opened in Philadelphia in 1754 as a precursor to the larger Merchants' Coffee House. These energetic new establishments were ridiculed as "seminaries of sedition" by British loyalists who viewed them as unsavory gathering places. Men came together in these coffeehouses to talk politics, make deals, catch up on the events of the day, and simply interact and share ideas—all while drinking coffee.[6]

It wasn't just Boston and Philadelphia where coffeehouse culture mirrored revolutionary fervor. In Williamsburg, Virginia, Richard Charlton's Coffeehouse became another cradle of political activity. On the front porch of Charlton's in 1765, an angry crowd of coffee patrons loudly confronted the royal tax collector, George Mercer, and chased him down Duke of Gloucester Street. After the dramatic encounter, he resigned his position.

The next time you visit colonial Williamsburg, after buying your kids muskets and tri-cornered hats so they'll stop whining, stop by Charlton's Coffeehouse. It's not the original, but a reconstruction on the same location was completed in 2009. For fun, you can order coffee and yell at British tourists.

The Military's Role in Popularizing Coffee

It's hard to imagine, but in the early days of America's military, soldiers received a daily ration of alcohol. I'm no five-star general, but loaded guns and whiskey just don't seem like a smart combination. In the early nineteenth century, while coffee's popularity among both soldiers and the general population ran hot, whiskey and rum remained in higher demand.

A decree issued by President Andrew Jackson that took effect on October 25, 1832, solidified coffee's standing in the United States. Recognizing that alcoholic rations had a less-than-desirable effect on the army's discipline and effectiveness (based on complaints from officers who served in the War of 1812), Jackson replaced the mandated daily rations of whiskey and rum with coffee and sugar. Popularizing coffee among the ranks, which eventually led to increased consumption in the general population, marked a huge step forward for coffee's mass appeal.[7]

During the Civil War, coffee became a major ingredient of the soldier's daily life. Until this time, coffee was seen more as a replacement or alternative to alcohol. "However, the act of drinking coffee during the Civil War became a ritual; it typically occurred among groups of soldiers huddled around the camp's fire. Gathering around the fire with strong hot coffee in hand discussing the day's events and their yearnings for home, created a sense of comfort and camaraderie."[8]

Or, as Union captain Robert K. Beecham wrote in a firsthand account of the Civil War published in 1911, titled *Gettysburg: The Pivotal Battle of the Civil War*, "The power of the soldiers to endure the fatigue of the march and keep their places in the ranks was greatly enhanced by an opportunity to brew a cup of coffee by the wayside."

Amazingly, in 1859 the Sharps Rifle Company began making a carbine with a hand-cranked grinder built into the gun stock. Union soldiers would fill the stock with coffee beans, grind them, and then dump them out to make coffee. Of course, as they were fighting to end slavery in America, they were simultaneously being fueled by coffee harvested by slaves in Brazil.

What truly iced America's taste for coffee was the confluence of major events of the early twentieth century: the Industrial Revolution, the rise of Madison Avenue's marketing machine, and World War I. Millions of American soldiers enjoyed coffee three times a day. When they returned home, the demand for coffee came with them.

By World War II, the average American serviceman was consuming 32.5 pounds of coffee per year.[9] That's a lot of coffee!

Speaking of World War II, it's believed, though not substantiated, that the term "caffè Americano" (American coffee) derives from the practice of American GIs serving in Italy. Upon encountering the strong, puts-hair-on-your-chest Italian espresso, they watered it down to make a similar drink to what they drank at home.

I've never really understood the concept of ordering an Americano (full disclosure: this is my brother Matt's coffee drink of choice so I'm kind of mocking him here). I mean, it's basically watered-down espresso for wimpy Americans who can't take the real stuff— the equivalent of adding ginger ale to single malt Scotch.

Anyway, if an "army marches on its stomach," as Napoleon suggested, the American military also soldiers on its coffee, and coffee's popularity in America is inextricably linked to military consumption.

Airborne!

Though not a coffee drinker during my army days, I love that the military played a role in popularizing coffee. For soldiers, coffee has long served as an important reminder of home during long deployments, evoking the familiar and offering reminders of the relationships that really matter. There may be no atheists in foxholes, but there are plenty of coffee drinkers.

A similar desire for comfort in the midst of adversity exists for every human being—it is not the exclusive domain of military personnel. We all reach for that metaphorical security blanket when in unfamiliar or trying circumstances. When we lose our sense of rootedness, disorientation takes hold, and we reach for what is familiar and comforting. We seek anchors to recall our very identity. For people of faith, this anchor is God. For Christians, Jesus calms the storm around us and within us.

It's not the only means, but when driven from our comfort zones, reaching for a cup of coffee can bring normalcy and offer solace. Sometimes God is made manifest in a cup of coffee, and situations abound in both military and civilian life where we find ourselves in places we could never have imagined, clinging to the familiar.

One such situation for me took place as a young ROTC cadet. In 1990, I found myself at Fort Benning, Georgia, having volunteered for Airborne School to train as a paratrooper. I was afraid of heights, so naturally I decided to jump out of airplanes.

To earn Airborne wings required making five parachute jumps. These were made after two weeks of ground training that included thousands of pushups in the sweltering August heat, learning how to properly land (it's the equivalent of jumping off a ten-foot wall), and instruction on exiting the aircraft via a training apparatus/torture device called the thirty-four-foot tower. Why thirty-four feet? Because army engineers had determined the precise height to maximize fear.

When you're actually up in the airplane and standing in the door, it's loud, windy, and unnerving. Suddenly the green light goes on, and you leap out into what feels like the abyss. We were taught to leap out rather than to just fall out, to avoid getting our lines caught in the giant propellers of that massive C-130. During those four long seconds before your parachute opens, you feel like a rag doll caught in a tornado.

To me, this is what life feels like when you enter a new and bewildering situation. Sometimes it takes you where you'd rather not go; sometimes it completely disorients you; sometimes its sheer force overwhelms you; sometimes it makes you feel utterly powerless.

After leaping out into that violent rush of wind and gaining separation from the airplane, when your chute opens up, the contrasting silence and peacefulness of the descent is remarkable. The ground rises rather quickly so you can't stay in this state of reverie for long. But then you rejoice in the old, familiar, taken-for-granted terra firma, as if encountering it for the first time. You take comfort in the recognizable terrain of the earth's crust and revel anew in its beauty. At least until you hear an Airborne instructor screaming at you to double-time it off the drop zone.

I still don't like heights, although I learned I can deal with them if I must. But what this experience brought into sharp relief for me was the necessity of being grounded in what matters and the comfort of the familiar, which, for many of us, may be a cup of coffee. I now understand how coffee brought this point home to American soldiers and sailors over the generations, and why we are all drawn to the familiar in moments of disruption and situations of uncertainty.

Instant Coffee and a Cup of Joe

So how did Americans go from drinking decent and flavorful coffee to scooping God-knows-how-old, pre-ground brown stuff out of giant tin cans?

World War I played a role here as well. As the war began and the soldier's insatiable thirst for coffee revealed itself as a key to military success, the army turned to a relatively new process of soluble coffee powder. While I consider the introduction of instant coffee a truly dark moment in history, the military encouraged the concept because it was easier to make and drink in the field.

In 1910, an enterprising immigrant with a patriotic name established the George Washington Coffee Refining Company in Brooklyn. Initially sold as Red E Coffee, the American government bought the instant-coffee product in mass quantities and shipped it to soldiers overseas once America entered the Great War. It became so indispensable to the soldiers they started fondly referring to it as drinking their "cup of George." One soldier wrote home, "I am very happy despite the rats, the rain, the mud, the draughts, the roar of the cannon and the scream of shells. It takes only a minute to light my little oil heater and make some George Washington Coffee. . . . Every night I offer up a special petition to the health and well-being of Mr. Washington."[10]

After the war ended, Washington's product remained popular, rebranded as "prepared coffee" for the home. "Went to war! Home again," read an advertisement with a saluting coffee can. By the time World War II started, the Swiss-based Nestlé corporation had devised a more efficient and effective method for producing instant coffee. Nescafé ended up dominating the marketplace, which foreshadowed the demise of the Washington Coffee Company. Washington sold his company just prior to his death in 1943 and the company went out of business in 1961.

It's intriguing that, in just a few years, soldiers transitioned from drinking a "cup of George" in World War I to a "cup of Joe" in World War II. As with many things involving coffee nomenclature, the reason is not entirely clear. Obviously, American soldiers were no longer literally drinking "George" during World War II, but such names often stick anyway. Some believe it refers to Josephus Daniels, secretary of the Navy from 1913 to 1921 under Woodrow Wilson, who banned alcoholic beverages onboard Navy vessels, making coffee the strongest drink in the ship's galley. However, it probably has more to do with the term "GI Joe" than anything else.

The Dumbing Down of the American Coffee Consumer

The rise of instant coffee did much to dumb down the taste buds of American coffee drinkers. You can point to mass production as a major culprit, as large companies sought consistency in taste over excellence. Welcome to 1950s America!

During the postwar years, most coffee came from cans of pre-ground beans and then got boiled beyond recognition in percolators. Coffee flowed in such a diluted state that it was often little more than brown water.

Incredibly, the high-water mark for coffee consumption in America was 1946 as, according to the Department of Agriculture, the average adult drank forty-eight gallons per year.[11] In comparison, the average American now consumes nineteen gallons of coffee every year. At first glance that's a stunning caffeination gap, though soda and energy drinks bring this down considerably. Still, that's leaving an awful lot of coffee in the carafe—especially when you consider that Finns top the modern consumption charts at thirty-eight gallons per year.

What's interesting about postwar coffee consumption, besides the dreadful flavor, is it was virtually all drip coffee. If you walked into a Brooklyn diner in October of 1955 with a hangover from celebrating the Dodgers' long-hoped-for World Series victory and ordered a macchiato or a cappuccino, the waitress would have looked at you as if you had three heads. Or at least as if you were speaking some peculiar foreign language. Specialty coffee didn't exist.

Coffee started its slow decline into the 1970s partly because of the clever marketing of soda. Cola companies employed celebrities to hawk their products while the coffee industry felt this was beneath the dignity of a drink that had been around for hundreds of years.

Astonishingly, given what we now know, soda companies promoted their products as healthful alternatives to coffee. Remember how your mother wouldn't let you drink coffee because it could "stunt your growth"? This was part of a campaign by soda companies to link coffee consumption to birth defects and heart disease. Current research has flip-flopped these findings, as most health-care professionals now consider coffee in moderation a key to a healthy lifestyle, while soda is linked to the nation's diabetes and obesity epidemics.

Coffee quality also declined when coffee companies began using cheap and inferior Robusta beans to lower production costs. As opposed to the more flavorful Arabica beans, Robusta beans grow at lower altitudes and are more disease- and pest-resistant due to the higher caffeine content. That's the good news. The bad news is they produce bitter-tasting coffee.

One of the main reasons for the bitter flavor, which cuppers describe in such technical terms as "rubbery" or like "burnt tires," is the higher caffeine content. Now, most of us might think this sounds like a good thing ("More caffeine! Better coffee!"), but we'd be wrong. Caffeine carries with it an astringent taste and Robusta beans have more than twice the caffeine of the average Arabica coffee (2.7 percent to 1.5 percent).

It also costs about half as much to harvest, so you can understand the temptation to use Robusta beans as coffee blend filler. In 1954, following a devastating frost in Brazil, Maxwell House began blending Robusta beans to lower costs. Other large coffee companies soon followed, and the dumbing down of coffee flavor continued unabated. You won't be surprised to learn that instant coffee consists of nearly 100 percent Robusta beans.

Decaf and the Rise of Sanka

Several years ago, a few clergy colleagues and purported friends sent me a small jar of Sanka. It was a joke of sorts, as I've been railing against the evils of Sanka for years. Few things make my stomach turn more than passing the ubiquitous orange packaging while browsing the coffee aisle at my local grocery store.

Decaffeinated coffee is bad enough. Whatever your theology about the underworld, we can all agree that *instant* decaf must be the work of the devil. To me, Sanka tastes like the bitter tears of Judas after realizing he just sold out the Savior of the world for thirty pieces of silver. I last drank it as a newly ordained cleric during a pastoral visit to an elderly parishioner's home. I was offered coffee as a genuine act of hospitality, which I gratefully accepted, only to realize with horror that she had made me a cup of Sanka. Since that time, I have always politely refused the offer of coffee whenever I visit someone in their home. I may be missing out on the greatest coffee ever brewed, but my Sanka PTSD is real.

Many people drink and enjoy decaffeinated coffee, and it accounts for a significant percentage of the coffee industry. Some drink it for medical reasons, others have a cup of decaf in the evening to prevent sleeplessness. The process of extracting caffeine from coffee beans resulted from an accidental discovery. In 1903, a German named Ludwig Roselius had a shipment of beans submerged in sea water and discovered that while the coffee flavor remained, most of the caffeine disappeared. Roselius patented the process, which involved steaming the beans and then using benzene as a solvent to remove the caffeine, in 1906. The caffeine-free beans were marketed throughout Europe via the Coffee Trading Company and sold in France as Sanka, derived from the French words *sans caféine* (without caffeine).

I'm not going to get into the science behind the decaffeination process, mostly because I don't care but also because I'm not a chemist. It has evolved over the years, with a number of high-quality decaffeinated coffees now available, and the relatively recent Swiss Water decaffeinating process is 100 percent chemical free.

Sanka became a huge brand in America when General Foods took over distribution in 1928. Robust marketing also played a major role in turning Sanka into a powerhouse in the coffee market. In the early 1950s and into the 1960s, Sanka was a regular sponsor of such popular television shows as *The Twilight Zone*, *The Andy Griffith Show*, and *I Love Lucy*. We also have Sanka to thank for making orange the universal color of decaf. Walk into any diner or restaurant and you know exactly which pot holds the decaf—the one with the bright orange handle.

That jar of Sanka I was given? I keep it in my office at church on my personal coffee preparation table next to my secret stash of the good stuff. It serves as a constant reminder that evil does indeed exist in this world and that rather than horns and a pitchfork, it comes in the form of a bright orange container.

Decaffeinated Faith

If you've ever tuned in to a TV preacher (or lost the remote and were too lazy to get up to change the channel), you've likely heard some guy with bad hair and a shiny suit railing against "decaffeinated faith." It's become a trope of sorts, a way of illustrating the point that *my* style of religion is full-test, while *yours* is weak and diluted.

There's little nuance in a faith presented in such stark, black-and-white terms and that always gives me pause. "You're either with me, or against me. You're either for God, or against God. You're either saved, or condemned."

Embedded in this archetype is a toxic masculinity where shades of gray are deemed effeminate and an introspective, contemplative approach to spirituality that leaves room for questioning and doubt is considered inadequate and fragile.

This isn't how God works, in my view—God exists in the midst of the questions! And while you won't catch me drinking decaffeinated coffee (unless it's after 5:00 p.m., an unfortunate consequence of middle age), I won't equate it with feebleness of spirit.

The my-way-or-the-highway approach to faith also places human limitations on God's sovereignty. Who's to say God doesn't speak to people in ways I can't hear or comprehend? The overwhelming hubris in imagining that I alone am the unfiltered receptor and interpreter of God's commandments is astounding. It also stifles authentic dialogue with people of different faith backgrounds. If I'm convinced of being 100 percent correct on issues of faith 100 percent of the time, that means whenever you disagree with my convictions, you are 100 percent wrong. Not a great starting point for cross-cultural conversation.

A few years ago, I passed along an image on Facebook that asked "How do you take your coffee?" It showed five coffee cups, labeled from A to E, with black on the left to barely brown on the right. People's responses overwhelmed me in terms of quantity and passion for their particular gradation. ("A all the way," "Team C!" "E or I drink tea"). It's not a bad metaphor for faith when you think about it. God speaks and we hear God's voice in a variety of ways. We may be zealous in our beliefs, but other avenues of discipleship abound. In other words, just because I drink black coffee doesn't mean I must compel you to do the same. That's not how faith, or coffee, works.

The Ubiquitous American "Coffee Break"

Okay, you've been reading this book for a while. Perhaps (probably?) you've even nodded off a bit. Well, wake up! It's time for a coffee break! Take fifteen minutes, pour yourself some coffee, stretch your legs, and then get back to the hard work of slogging through the remaining chapters.

Alright. Welcome back. I hope you enjoyed your coffee break, as integral a piece of American life as halftime at a football game. You may assume the concept simply arose as an organic part of the American workday. But no, it's a bit more contrived than that.

The coffee break as we know it was the brainstorm of one man, a psychologist named J. B. Watson.[12] Trained in the tradition of behaviorism, Watson and his colleagues believed people could be guided to react in predictable ways through repetitive actions. This classic conditioning led Pavlov's dog to salivate every time he heard a bell rung.

When Watson left academia, he worked for an advertising agency that sought to put these principles to work selling products to the American consumer. He made a fortune hawking Camel cigarettes and Johnson's Baby Powder, among other well-known products, with his partner James Webb Young, a former evangelical door-to-door Bible salesman. The cynical person might consider Johnson's techniques brainwashing. But I guess one person's brainwashing is another's brilliant marketing scheme.

In time, Watson worked on an advertisement for Maxwell House Coffee that helped ingrain the coffee break into the American psyche. It would be disingenuous to claim that Watson invented the coffee break. More accurately, he popularized and normalized it as a regular and accepted part of the workday.

As industrialized coffee became an essential part of the postwar climate, employers saw the benefit of their workers getting a quick pick-me-up before "getting back to work!" The first coffee vending machines began to appear in office break rooms. Invented by former military engineer Cyrus Melikian in 1946, Kwik Kafes dispensed a hot cup of coffee in three minutes using hot water and a liquid coffee concentrate.

This was basically caffeinated swill, but it did the trick, and soon enough such inferior brews became the norm. I'd consider this period in American history the dark ages of coffee culture—though I don't mean dark in a good, coffee kind of way.

The Green Elephant in the Room

Starbucks says they are going to start putting religious quotes on cups. The very first one will say, "Jesus! This cup is expensive!"

—Conan O'Brien, comedian

You can't talk about coffee without acknowledging the impact Starbucks has had on the global coffee industry. Well, you could, but you'd be ignoring the giant, caffeinated elephant in the room. Whether you're a Starbucks devotee with the app on your phone and a branded travel mug in your hand or someone who actively avoids the corporate chain, everyone has an opinion about the Seattle-based coffee behemoth.

Starbucks is one of the most polarizing brands on the planet. Some coffee drinkers seem to wrap their identity up in the familiar logo while others regularly visit the plethora of anti-Starbucks websites out there to post their over-caffeinated screeds.

If one drink symbolizes the mixed reactions to Starbucks, it's the Pumpkin Spice Latte. Starting in late summer, the marketing blitz begins. Like seasonal Christmas creep (it's not even Halloween yet!), PSL season seems to start earlier and earlier. Personally speaking, I don't appreciate images of wool scarves and cozy fireplaces when I'm mowing my lawn in 95-degree weather, but I have friends who pine for the return of the PSL like autumn-crazed lunatics staring up at their still-green elm trees waiting for the first leaves to fall.

I just despise the sickeningly sweet taste. And the fact that actual pumpkin doesn't exist in the *Pumpkin* Spice Latte. And the $4.50 price tag. But I admit to being a PSL curmudgeon. If that's your thing, enjoy it. Just know that you've encountered the crossroads of the love-it-or-hate-it relationship so many people have with Starbucks.

Game Changer

Whatever you think about some of the sugary how-can-you-even-call-that-coffee drinks on the Starbucks menu, the company has transformed the coffee industry. As Mike Love of Coffee Labs put it when I asked him about the omnipresent coffee giant, "If it weren't for Starbucks, I wouldn't be here." He meant that Starbucks paved the way for independent coffee shops like the one he owns. Starbucks helped revolutionize the coffee scene in the United States, and for that, no matter what you think about the corporate culture behind half-caf soy caramel macchiatos, we should all be grateful.

Starbucks changed the coffee game by importing coffeehouse culture from Italy while simultaneously getting consumers used to paying what in the mid-1980s and early 1990s seemed like exorbitant prices for coffee. They helped consumers realize that what they thought was coffee was actually a bitter, watered-down version of what could be an amazing culinary experience.

In Starbucks lore, the revolution began in 1982 when Starbucks' marketing director Howard Schultz went to Italy on a coffee-buying excursion. While in Rome, he noticed the coffee shops on every corner selling quality espresso drinks amid comfortable gathering spaces. He returned to Seattle convinced this model was the coffee wave of the future. Unfortunately, or fortunately if you're a current Starbucks shareholder, the three original founders didn't share Schultz's vision.

A few years later when Starbucks was put up for sale, Schultz jumped at the opportunity, and the original owners collectively became the Fifth Beatle of the coffee industry. By 1989, Schultz had opened forty-six stores in the Northwest and upper Midwest, and the aggressive expansion never stopped.

One critical piece of the concept that resonated with consumers was the rise of the so-called *third space*. Starbucks offered a space away from home and work where people could relax with friends, enjoy some time alone, or just sit in a comfortable chair with an indulgent beverage. Yes, the coffee part was an important innovation, but the environment was equally critical to Starbucks' early success.

Think about what you see when you walk into a Starbucks: friends breezily chatting over coffee, a writer banging away on a laptop, a business meeting in progress, someone sitting on a sofa listening to music and enjoying the free Wi-Fi. You may see these same things when you walk into any coffee shop these days, but fewer third spaces existed before Starbucks came along and inspired and invigorated the concept in the United States. Several key elements create this welcoming space, and Starbucks executives don't leave the ambience to chance. It's supposed to feel thrown together, but a tremendous amount of market research and designer hours have gone into creating these spaces. The aroma of freshly ground coffee, comfy leather couches, soft music, calming color schemes, cozy nooks. Entering a Starbucks feels warm and inviting because it was designed precisely with that concept in mind. Contrived or not, it's why we can credit Starbucks with the ascent of modern coffeehouse culture.

The Mothership

Full disclosure: I've always had a love/hate relationship with Starbucks. Okay, mostly a hate/hate relationship because I just don't enjoy their coffee. I understand how they played an integral role in shaping American coffee culture, but I don't appreciate darkly roasted coffee served at scalding temperatures. Not my thing. So I admit to being slightly wary of, if grateful for, the invitation to visit the Starbucks mothership in Seattle.

While you can simply wander into one of nearly thirty thousand Starbucks worldwide, you can't just show up at Starbucks headquarters and expect to gain admittance to their corporate offices.

Fortunately, a parishioner of mine works with Starbucks in some vague financial services industry capacity, and he pulled a few strings to get me a tour.

My childhood friend Kevin Daniels, who moved to Seattle from Baltimore nearly twenty-five years ago, joined me on this excursion. He's become a coffee aficionado himself over the years, although I was surprised to learn he doesn't wear plaid shirts every day and listen exclusively to concert bootlegs of Nirvana. But it was great having a local and trusted guide join me on my adventure to the ground zero of the American coffee revolution.

Pulling up to the corporate headquarters is impressive in itself. Housed in a massive red brick building constructed in 1912 in Seattle's industrial district, it was formerly owned by Sears, Roebuck and Company. Rechristened the Starbucks Center in 1997, it's topped by a clock tower over which looms the top half of the familiar green mermaid in a sort of Kilroy Was Here vibe. While most independent coffee shops are run out of a small back office in shouting distance from the whir of the espresso machine's steam wand, that's not how Starbucks operates. Starbucks brews a unique blend of corporate and coffee culture.

Following proper vetting and the issuing of official visitor badges, Kevin and I were met by Tom Shaw, Starbucks' vice-president for investor relations, and Ann-Marie Kurtz, the company's manager of global coffee. Ann-Marie started her career as a Starbucks barista in 1990 and has worked for the company ever since. Her title may as well be Starbucks Coffee Czar, as she is a fount of all things Starbucks, from corporate history to the effects of climate change on the global coffee industry to the company's charitable endeavors.

The corporate loyalty displayed by everyone we encountered was astonishing. I won't reference Kool-Aid, since we're speaking of coffee and want no negative connotation, but people who work at Starbucks are passionate about both coffee and the company's mission. Starbucks remains uniquely qualified and positioned to influence the global coffee industry, and they take that responsibility seriously.

What amazed me most was visiting the employees-only, fully staffed Starbucks nestled in between the offices. From human resources managers to executive secretaries to bean counters (not *those* beans) to quality-control tasters, this is a well-caffeinated work

Watching my coffee being brewed on the Clover machine at the employees-only Starbucks at the Seattle headquarters.

force. Granted I couldn't help but think about the poor baristas who had to work there. They were friendly, highly competent, and probably the crème de la crème of the barista population, but it induced nightmares of having to preach to a church full of pastors. Not that coffee folks would be as judgmental as fellow clergy, but still!

Don't tell anyone, but in addition to the regular Starbucks menu items, the in-house operation also offers special coffees not available in the regular stores. I had a Nicaraguan single-origin coffee expertly brewed on an $11,000 Clover brewing machine, which is basically like a French press in reverse without the nasty grounds getting into the cup. Or as Ann-Marie put it to me as I stared in rapt wonder at the Clover in action, it's like "drinking coffee in high definition." And it was.

Starbucks is unlike any other coffee company in the world in terms of its market share, number of employees, and sheer volume of coffee sourced, roasted, brewed, and served. Yes, they maintain their status as a hugely profitable global corporation. You may or may not love their coffee, you may or may not love their methods, but there are people from Howard Schultz on down trying to make a difference in the lives of those up and down the coffee supply chain, and I was immensely grateful for this unique look at the operation.

Reserve Roastery

After bidding farewell to our gracious hosts, Kevin and I made our way to the new Starbucks Reserve Roastery and Tasting Room in Seattle's vibrant Capitol Hill neighborhood. I was particularly keen to visit the Roastery, as even battle-hardened coffee-industry professionals speak glowingly about the place's sleek design and technological prowess.

Starbucks has opened several of these new concept stores in various markets throughout the world. The original one is in Seattle, naturally, on the famous Pike Street, just nine blocks from the original Starbucks.

The Reserve Roastery is many things: pilgrimage site for Starbucks lovers; mind-blowing coffee experience for people enamored with different brewing techniques like siphons and pour-overs and unique coffee drinks not available at your neighborhood Starbucks; technological wonder with massive roasting machines tended to by guys with huge beards and handlebar mustaches; laboratory with ornate cold-brew systems that look like something out of the mind of a mad scientist; coffee museum with displays about coffee-growing regions and processing techniques. Imagine the coffee equivalent of a mashup between Walt Disney World and Studio 54 and you get the idea.

The concept behind the Reserve Roastery stores is to return to what Howard Schultz talks about as the "theater of coffee." These are meant to be destinations, not drive-throughs; places that emphasize coffee as an experience not just a caffeine fix. I think there's also an attempt to bring in consumers who feel Starbucks has gotten away from its original core commitment to quality coffee. The Reserve concept seeks to introduce consumers to a rotating array of small-lot coffees from places like Ethiopia, Jamaica, Brazil, and Guatemala. A major educational goal connects coffee drinkers with particular farms and farmers in ways that can't happen when you order a Blonde Roast or Pike's Place, which blends coffees from farms all over the world.

As with everything Starbucks, just as many people will flock to the Reserve Roasteries as will condemn them. And in the end, Starbucks stockholders will be rewarded.

Red Cup Controversy

Not just any coffee company can so powerfully impact American society that it finds itself in the midst of the political culture wars. But that's exactly what happened when the famed Red Cup controversy reared its caffeinated head. In 2015, Starbucks changed its annual holiday-themed cup to a plain, festive bright red with the circular green mermaid logo. Red and green—Santa colors. A cute, simple design meant to put everyone in the holiday spirit as they ordered their calorie-laden peppermint latte, right? Not so fast, Christmas hater!

After removing the traditional Christmas symbols like snowmen, trees, ornaments, and snowflakes of past years' cup designs, suddenly Starbucks was Exhibit A in the War on Christmas. One rather unhinged internet evangelist put together a YouTube video in which he commented, "Starbucks REMOVED CHRISTMAS from their cups because they hate Jesus . . . SO I PRANKED THEM . . . and they HATE IT!!!!" He "pranked" them by ordering a cup of coffee and telling the barista his name was Merry Christmas. So the Starbucks employee dutifully wrote "Merry Christmas" on his cup.

In other words, his prophetic protest meant supporting the company he professed to abhor by buying their product and giving them publicity. And, not for nothing, but it's not as if Starbucks suddenly removed Christian iconography from their holiday cups. Jesus, Mary, Joseph, John the Baptist, et al. weren't being banished. Generic, non-scriptural snowmen were.

This whole absurd episode shed more light upon the state of our divided country—and internet-fueled outrage—than it did on an alleged anti-Christian movement. It does show just how iconic Starbucks has become, however. A coffee shop becoming a catalyst for talk-radio folderol? That's impressive.

Believe it or not, this contrived controversy wasn't even the first time a dispute arose over Starbucks Christmas coffee. In 1997, Starbucks attorneys contacted the abbot of a tiny Russian Orthodox monastery (tiny as in five monks in residence) on Vashon Island in Puget Sound. The issue at hand revolved around a coffee-roasting monk at All-Merciful Savior Monastery who raised money for his order by selling a coffee called Christmas Blend. Starbucks had recently trademarked the term and insisted the monk cease and desist his operation. Once the David and Goliath story hit the national news, Starbucks backed off, rightly seeing a publicity nightmare in the offing. You can still purchase the holiday Christmas Blend from the monastery from October through December.

A Different Nirvana

Before Seattle put itself on the musical map with grunge, the mid-1980s alternative rock subgenre that spurred a global movement, it had already claimed a stake as the center of the gourmet coffee world. Kurt Cobain and his Nirvana bandmates, Pearl Jam, Soundgarden, and the rest were surely fueled by substances beyond coffee, but a

Venn diagram would show throngs of their Seattle-based fans also enamored with high-end coffee.

Many people don't realize that the smaller Peet's Coffee not only predates Starbucks but that the late Alfred Peet played a major role in launching both specialty coffee and the global phenomenon that is Starbucks. Sure, Peet's Coffee is now owned by JAB Holding Company, a Luxembourg-based German conglomerate that also owns Panera Bread, Snapple, Bruegger's Bagels, Caribou Coffee, Krispy Kreme, Keurig Green Mountain, Stumptown Coffee, and many other well-known brands in the fast food, luxury fashion, and consumer goods industries. But Alfred Peet founded it as Peet's Coffee and Tea in 1966 in Berkeley, California, and industry insiders point to this as the seminal moment in the coffee revolution, bridging the gap between the 1950s weak, mass-produced diner coffee and today's specialty coffee world.

Peet, who died in 2007 at the age of eighty-seven, was a Dutchman who learned to roast coffee from his father, operator of a small roastery in the years before World War II. Dismayed by the lack of decent coffee when he emigrated to San Francisco in 1955, he eventually opened his own shop. In many ways, Peet took the greatest pride in introducing people to coffee's potential as a transformative experience. He was also generous with his time in teaching the art and craft of roasting to those eager to learn. Among his disciples were three men who would change the course of coffee history. Jerry Baldwin, Zev Siegel, and Gordon Bowker, who met as students at the University of San Francisco, learned roasting at the feet of the Dutch master, and then took that technique to Seattle and opened the first Starbucks in 1971 in Pike's Place Market.

Coffee aficionados speak of the coffee revolution in terms of waves. Not like one giant, scalding tidal wave of single-origin Sumatran goodness washing over you, but as in a series of phases. The big deal here is the so-called third wave in which coffee is viewed as a culinary delight. The third wave has been a long time coming, but in order to comprehend the farm-to-cup craft-brewing world in which independent coffee shops now exist, you need to go back in time to what coffee once was.

We've already explored some of this, but the wave theory helps put it all into context. The first wave traces its roots back to the 1800s and culminated in the post–World War II 1950s. It emphasized convenience, affordability, and mass consumption at the expense of quality and taste. In this era, many of the brands we know and, well, not necessarily love, came into being: Folgers, Maxwell House, Nescafé. It's also identified with those giant vacuum-sealed tin cans, percolators, diners, and mediocre-at-best coffee.

The second wave was a reaction to the uninspired coffee experience and the realization that a better way existed. This phase can be directly linked to Peet's but is most closely identified with the rise of Starbucks. The term *specialty coffee* emerges, and people now see that not all beans—or coffee—are created equal. Previously unheard-of terms like latte, espresso, and Frappuccino enter the American lexicon, along with concepts like the French Press and paying stiff prices for coffee drinks in shops specifically designed as meeting places.

First coined in the early 2000s, the concept of a third wave of coffee became defined by the growth of independent coffee shops. In America, the big three were Intelligentsia Coffee & Tea in Chicago, Counter Culture Coffee in North Carolina, and Stumptown

Coffee Roasters in Portland, but the whole movement was buttressed by smaller independent shops that popped up around the country. These new purveyors of specialty coffee were passionate, driven by the desire to educate coffee drinkers by opening up a new world of quality, and concerned with ethical and environmental justice.

When you walk into your local independent coffee shop, however, please don't go up to the barista and say, "Wow! You guys are really riding the third wave!" If the phrase is uttered out loud, the magic evaporates.

Coffee Crawl

If you've ever been a twentysomething, you've likely experienced a pub crawl. You know, going from bar to bar, having a pint of ale or a shot of tequila, and then heading to the next destination on your increasingly fuzzy map.

In Seattle, as in an ever-growing number of urban areas, you can sign up for a coffee crawl. The good news, vis-à-vis a pub crawl, is you spend a higher percentage of your time not throwing up. At my insistence, Kevin and I signed up for one that left from the Seattle Art Museum on a typical drizzly Saturday in Seattle.

One of the first things you notice when walking around Seattle, besides the 142 Starbucks locations, is the sheer volume of available coffee. Shops, street carts, wholesalers, trucks holding up traffic to unload burlap sacks of beans. Before I arrived, I thought the notion that the entire city was coffee crazed might have been overplayed, but evidently not. This place takes its coffee as seriously as it takes its ethically sourced, free-range chicken. Or maybe that's Portland. Anyway,

Decked out in plaid for the Seattle coffee crawl.

there's a coffee shop on every corner, and they never lack for clientele, seemingly at any hour of the day. Market saturation seems to be an ephemeral concept taught in Intro to Economics classes at the University of Washington, and absolutely theoretical when it comes to

Seattle's coffee culture. If I started selling coffee out of the trunk of my rental car, I swear there'd be a line around the block within minutes.

Our coffee crawl was led by a young woman named Val who works for an outfit called Seattle by Foot. She did a masterful job keeping an increasingly caffeinated group of ten from falling into an open manhole or wandering off into one of the many Starbucks we passed along the way. We tasted a number of different coffees—some single-origins, some blends—along with a latte and a shot of espresso.

Val explained each coffee and brewing method as we popped in and out of cafés, with a bit of history about the particular shop tossed in to spice things up. I thought I demonstrated heroic self-restraint in not sharing all the photos from my recent trip to the coffee farms in Central America and being that jerk know-it-all who tends to show up on such tours. Though I balanced this by wearing a plaid shirt, since what else would you wear while on a Seattle coffee tour?

One of the things I learned spending time in Seattle, touring Starbucks, and going on the coffee crawl is that people generally like their coffee dark and strong. My favorite coffee on the crawl was at Caffe Ladro, partly because it stood out as particularly flavorful and partly because it wasn't over-roasted to my tastes. It didn't hurt that it was grown and processed by a cooperative of women farmers in southern Rwanda.

West Coast Roasts

It took going to Seattle to understand exactly why I've never been a fan of darker-roasted coffee. Dark roasts are by far the most popular roasts in the United States. Much of this has to do with Starbucks, as they were influenced by the darker Italian roasts when they took higher-quality coffee to the masses. The majority of coffee shops in Seattle have traditionally followed this formula—this was certainly the case on the coffee crawl. There's a reason people refer to this darker style of coffee roasting as the West Coast roast.

High-quality beans—beans grown at high elevation, hand-picked only when ripe, and so forth—naturally have more flavor. A lighter roast brings out the flavor of the beans in amazing ways. If you took highly prized beans and dark roasted them, they would lose their subtlety and end up tasting pretty much like any other coffee. The difference between high-quality and low-quality beans narrows dramatically the longer the beans remain in the roaster.

To me, most dark roasted coffee just tastes like coffee. Not deeply flavorful, subtle, sweet coffee, but kind of a generic, woodsy coffee taste. For many people, that's precisely what they're looking for, and I totally get that. But on my own coffee journey, I've learned that I crave the flavors of delicate single-origin, craft coffee. I don't *think* I'm turning into an obnoxious, judgmental, snobby coffee guy, I just prefer lighter-roasted coffees.

I'm also convinced that many people believe darker, stronger, bolder coffee has more caffeine. "Give me the strongest coffee you've got! I have a lot to do today!" This is actually not true—lighter roasts have a higher caffeine content because the beans are denser than dark roasts.

Besides being influenced initially by the (dark) Italian roasts, coffee processed on the scale of a Starbucks has to be darkly roasted in order to guarantee uniformity of flavor. When you purchase that grande Verona blend at the Starbucks in Seattle, you want it to taste just like the Verona you ordered at the airport in Boston before you boarded the plane. Starbucks simply can't offer that consistency if they are lightly roasting and then blending coffees from all over the world.

The thing is, you really don't know where the coffee you drink at Starbucks comes from. There are many regions from which they buy coffee, but I'm talking about the beans in your Frappuccino or your Pike's Place. The beans in one drink may come from five different countries. Who knows? The coffee guys at Starbucks don't care, really, as long as the flavor profile is consistent. This isn't a knock on Starbucks, it's just the reality of a company that makes over four billion cups of coffee each year. For coffee lovers who care where their coffee comes from, Starbucks is seeking to address this with their Reserve coffees, but the effectiveness won't be known for some time. Again, the sheer scale and pursuit of brand consistency works against the quality.

In speaking with some disappointingly-not-as-surly-as-I-would-have-expected baristas at a few of the newer (i.e., post-Starbucks) coffee shops in Seattle, the third-wave lighter roasts are increasingly popular around town. While the vast majority of coffee sold and consumed in Seattle continues to be dark roasts, room exists for a variety of tastes even in the heart of the American coffee renaissance. But that's the joy of coffee: there is not one monolithic way to do it correctly. My own preferences continue to develop, as I hope yours do. And that's the joy of the journey.

Compline at St. Mark's

On my last night in Seattle I attended the service of compline at St. Mark's Cathedral. It was a beautiful evening and I decided to walk the three miles from my downtown hotel to the Capitol Hill neighborhood. Or perhaps I was just over-caffeinated and needed to work off some extra energy before the 10:00 p.m. Sunday evening liturgy.

If you aren't familiar with compline (pronounced *komp'-lin*), it's rooted in the tradition of monastic night prayers. At St. Mark's, this haunting, achingly beautiful service is led by an all-male choir chanting ancient texts amid candlelight. Compline at St. Mark's has become wildly popular, drawing all sorts and conditions of people, from University of Washington students who spread blankets out on the floor so they can enter fully into the meditative nature of the experience to tourists, to the homeless, to people of all faiths. We all had in common a yearning to glory in the presence of something greater than ourselves.

For me, this takes the form of encounter with Jesus Christ, whose presence I felt deeply and tangibly that evening. Others may have been there to simply soak in the peaceful ambience and enjoy a respite from the pace and volume of frenzied lives. Most were likely on a continuum of sorts, but that's the way of seekers after the divine.

The journey metaphor easily slips into cliché, yet it abounds with profound truth. As I have entered my own coffee journey through this book, the parallels to the excursion of faith have reverberated. The big tent of the coffee world, where room exists for a variety of tastes and flavors and personalities, resembles the diverse religious connection of worshippers at the cathedral compline service. Some search for the next hot trend and others remain content to stick with their usual. It's easy to judge and label those whose views don't mimic our own—I've been guilty of this from both a faith and a coffee perspective. And every time I catch myself in this mindset, I recognize how it limits my view of self and of others, one that celebrates differ-ence while recognizing us all as distinctively and beautifully unique.

Letting go of these micro-judgments is freeing, and that's what the stunningly beautiful service of compline illustrated for me that night in Seattle. We're all on this journey together, at different stages, leading down different paths. In the midst of my own coffee journey, this was a critical reminder that we are all pilgrims on the journey of life and faith. And being armed with a good cup of coffee, however you define it, is a good and joyful thing.

Coffeehouse Culture

Why do our men trifle away their time, scald their chops,
and spend their money, all for a little base, black, thick,
nasty, bitter, stinking, nauseous, puddle water?

—1674 Women's Petition Against Coffee

love coffee shops. Everything about them. The aroma, the sound of milk being steamed, the creative types drawn to them, the buzz of conversation, the clatter of mugs being cleared, talking coffee minutiae with the passionate baristas. A well-appointed, independent coffee shop is my happy place. And that's coming from someone who can't stand that vapid phrase.

Now that there are so many outstanding coffee shops in our midst, we tend to take them for granted. But they didn't spontaneously appear. A rich history exists that offers insights into today's coffeehouse culture, and it's fun to pull back the layers between the first coffeehouses and that new one that just opened around the corner from your office.

The Rise of the Coffeehouse

As debate over the religious legality of coffee continued in the Muslim world, it became intertwined with the concept of the coffeehouse. With its increasing popularity, the consumption of coffee became secularized and no longer remained the sole domain of the devout. Hospitality and conversation migrated from places of worship to the home to the coffeehouse, and this had powerful social implications. Strangers and people of different backgrounds could now congregate, and the stimulating effects of coffee only aided intellectual rigor and allowed people to stay in conversation into the night.

Coffee became so popular that the first coffeehouses, known as *Kaveh Kanes*, opened around Mecca in the fifteenth century. The cultural and social impact of these new establishments cannot be overstated, as they were among the first public places where people could gather socially to discuss religious and political matters.

Not everyone was thrilled with this development since these spots threatened the more conservative elements of society, including the religious establishment and the monarchy. In their eyes, the spread of coffee culture distracted the faithful and led to potential sedition among the populace. By this time, coffee had come to be identified as the drink of Islam, yet it wasn't until the Ottoman Empire's influence in Constantinople that coffeehouse culture fully flourished.

The Ottoman chronicler İbrahim Peçevi reports the opening of the first coffeehouse in Istanbul: "Until the year 962 (1554–55), in the High, God-Guarded city of Constantinople, as well as in Ottoman lands generally, coffee and coffeehouses did not exist. About that year, a fellow called Hâkem (Hakam) from Aleppo and a wag called Sems (Shams) from Damascus, came to the city: they each opened a large shop in the district called Tahtakale, and began to purvey coffee."[1]

Although coffeehouses were known in Persia, the ones opened by these two men were the first truly secular coffeehouses. Many Sufis, so closely linked to and responsible for early coffee culture, complained about the defamation of the pious aura surrounding their coffee rituals by idle chitchat, cheap entertainment, and unholy conversation.

This new, more social gathering over coffee threatened the ruling authorities and led to a second wave of coffee suppression based on the fear of sedition rather than Islamic law. This is what drove the brutal persecution of coffee drinkers under Sultan Murad IV.

From these humble beginnings, the coffeehouse concept went viral. According to historical accounts, by 1566 there were six hundred coffeehouses in Constantinople, though, shockingly, not a single one was named Starbucks.[2]

What would you have encountered in one of these sixteenth-century Turkish coffeehouses? Just like today's multifaceted culinary culture, the experiences varied widely, from humble kiosks amid busy marketplaces to sumptuous, shaded gardens overlooking the Bosporus. The coffee was brewed in large cauldrons and often enhanced with spices such as cardamom, saffron, or ambergris (expensive whale vomit). The high-end coffeehouses were adorned with divans, carpets, fountains, beautiful serving girls, poets, and singers.

You could even hire your own personal *kaveghi* to attend to all your coffee needs. The sultan and other wealthy members of society had a *kaveghi* on payroll at their homes. In addition to procuring, brewing, and serving coffee, this at-home barista would be responsible for the care of all the household's coffee cups and vessels. And I'm pretty sure I need one.

Emancipated from the exclusive realm of religion, coffee fueled intellectual debate, and coffeehouses became significant venues for the promotion of commerce and the discussion of political events. Socially, they helped move the sense of community beyond the home and into the public sphere.

The European Coffeehouse: London

Europe experienced a similar renaissance once coffee began its rapid spread across the continent. Coffee first came through the Italian port city of Venice sometime in the sixteenth century. At first, the "Wine of Araby" was used for medicinal purposes and then as an exclusive and exotic quaff for the upper classes.

The first coffeehouse in England opened in 1651, in Oxford, under the aegis of an enterprising man known to history as Jacob the Jew.[3] Two years later, the first coffeehouse in London was unveiled, and by 1715 coffee drinkers could choose from one of two thousand coffeehouses in London alone.[4]

Teeming with people from different classes, these coffeehouses played a novel and important role in a society traditionally bound by rigid class strictures. They quickly became social centers allowing for the civil exchange of diverse points of view—unlike the ubiquitous taverns, a difference of opinion over coffee didn't lead to a drunken brawl. In fact, these early coffeehouses became known in England as "penny universities" based on the entrance fee and the informal education they provided.

As the debate raged over the benefits—medical and otherwise—of coffee, the ubiquitous post-Gutenberg pamphleteers sprang into action. One amusing exchange began with a bawdy 1674 broadside titled *The Women's Petition against Coffee.* In this anonymous tract, women complained about the hours their men were spending in coffeehouses. Yet the real thrust was that coffee was making English men unable to satisfy their wives in bed. The women wrote of the "enfeebling, heathenish liquor called coffee," which, after drinking it, left their men "with nothing moist but their snotty Noses, nothing stiffe but their Joints, nor standing but their Ears."[5]

Of course the men offered a tongue-in-cheek reply with *The Men's Answer to the Women's Petition against Coffee.* The masculine reply highlighted the benefits of the new habit, argued that coffee did not make them impotent, vindicated their performance between the sheets, and contended that coffee actually dried up the "Crude Flatulent Humours" that made husbands fart in bed.[6] So much for the highbrow image of genteel Londoners sipping tea.

The burgeoning middle class also used coffeehouses as places of commerce. In his seventeenth-century coffeehouse, Edward Lloyd posted maritime schedules for his seafaring patrons who came for coffee, gossip, and news of shipping routes. The world-famous insurance company Lloyd's of London emerged out of this mercantile coffeehouse.

One group delighted at the rise of coffee culture might surprise you: the Puritans. Not exactly known for embracing new things, religious leaders rejoiced that coffee was replacing ale as the primary beverage of the nation. Coffeehouses supplanting pubs as the social center of communal life was a major breakthrough in a nation where public drunkenness was something of an epidemic. There's no question this new sobering energy drink fit in nicely with the puritanical Protestant work ethic.

Dens of Sedition

Whether it is the drink itself or a combination of coffee paired with conversation, coffeehouses have often raised suspicions from the ruling authorities. As we've seen with the early coffeehouses in the Muslim world, religious and secular authorities were distrustful of their subjects gathering under such conditions.

No doubt subversive and rebellious thoughts bubbled up in taverns and alehouses over the ages. Alcohol didn't lead to cogent, well-thought-out action, however. Coffeehouses? Now *that's* where revolution is plotted and carried out. In America, the radical Sons of Liberty planned the Boston Tea Party of 1773 in The Green Dragon Coffeehouse. In France, the mob that stormed the Bastille in 1789 first met at Café Foy. Is coffee a radical drink? Does the clear-thinking and energetic qualities of coffee really bring down kings and expose tyrants? It's hard to argue otherwise. Surely the downfall of plenty of clergy has taken place during post-worship coffee-hour gossip in parish halls all over the world.

Coffeehouse Identity

There exists a powerful sense of identity and loyalty that comes with your regular coffee spot. I'm very passionate about the two coffee shops that have fueled my creative energies over the past twenty years: Coffee Labs Roasters in Tarrytown, New York, and Redeye Roasters in Hingham, Massachusetts. You can't get through this book without hearing me go on *ad nauseam* about these places and their owners, and when you think of coffee shops you likely have similar feelings about your own favorite spots.

Coffee shops sell T-shirts and mugs with their logos for a reason—people buy them. I keep pens and pencils on my desk in a vintage mug sporting the old Coffee Labs logo (they've since rebranded). I have a purple Redeye Roasters T-shirt with God—Guts—Coffee emblazoned across the front sitting in my dresser at home.

I buy these things partly because they support the small businesses I'm so fond of and partly, if I'm honest, because I want to be associated with and connected to the broader coffee culture. Fantasies aside, I'm not a coffee farmer or roaster or barista or café owner. I don't have a fertile mountain in Guatemala; I'd burn myself if I tried roasting coffee; any latte art I produced would be rather . . . abstract. I'm keeping my day job.

My connection to coffee culture, in other words, comes exclusively through the cup I pay for at my local coffee shop or the beans

I purchase online. It's enhanced through relationships I have developed with people in the coffee industry over the years, and I value those friendships. For the most part, however, I am a coffee layman. I'm fine with that on most days, but loyalty ultimately lies in relationship with the people whose coffee I enjoy, and that's the connection I most crave.

Customer loyalty isn't something new. Businesses have sought ways to cultivate consumer allegiance for generations. Coffee elicits particular passions, and the places you buy it create connections in ways that transcend, say, the spot you bring your car for an oil change. No one proudly wears their Jiffy Lube shirt around town to underscore their taste in motor oil or lube jobs. Yet we love showing up to meetings with our insulated, branded hot cup to show the world we are environmentally conscious *and* a purveyor of fine coffee *and* not beholden to corporate America (unless it's a Starbucks product, which it likely is).

I know some Starbucks devotees who so passionately love the brand that, whenever they travel, the first thing they do is mark out all the locations on their smartphones. Of course, that's not hard with Starbucks as you encounter one the moment you exit the aircraft and step into the terminal.

Here in Boston, it's all about Dunkin' Donuts. I may not drink the stuff, but my kids love the place. Ben and Zak are all about the iced mocha latte, even in mid-January when the snowdrifts reach the first-floor window sills. And I wouldn't dare trash talk Dunkies around the guy who plows the church parking lot when it snows. Loyalty runs deep.

Denominational loyalty can be equally entrenched. I don't sport an Episcopal shield tattoo (or, full disclosure, any tattoo), but I know people who do. I have Lutheran friends who love wearing their Martin Luther "Nailed It" T-shirts while grocery shopping. I've seen plenty of Follow Me to XX Church bumper stickers on cars that just cut me off on the I-95 exit ramp. Such loyalties may announce joyful affiliations, even if they don't bode well for the prospect of Christian unity.

Brand loyalty, whether it's coffee- or faith-based, can blind us to the inherent gifts of others. Tunnel vision keeps us from seeing beyond our own bubbles, and we miss nuance and texture that may elevate our respective experiences. Go ahead and purchase that Death Wish Coffee travel mug. Buy the Hug a Methodist apron. Just remember to remain open to possibilities and experiences that broaden your worldview rather than limit it.

Coffee Shop as Satellite Office

I spend a lot of time in coffee shops. This isn't an earth-shattering revelation to anyone who knows me or follows me on Twitter. But it's not just to hang out and soak in the hip, coffee-flavored vibe; though there is that. The coffee shop serves as my satellite office, a place where I go to write sermons, articles, books, and blog posts; a spot to meet parishioners and interact with strangers.

I joke about it, but at the heart of coffee culture is building community, and from my perch at Redeye Roasters I plan and plot church events and engage in moments of profound pastoral care. In very real ways, the body of Christ that is the church is built up one steaming mug of coffee at a time.

I hold informal weekly office hours called "Redeye with the Rector" that include an open-door policy and no agenda. Some weeks are busier than others, but every time I do this, I have an in-depth conversation with at least one person I normally wouldn't have a chance to encounter in a meaningful way. I very much see the coffee shop as a place of inspiration, interaction, and interplay.

But mostly I write. One of the reasons I go out to write, besides the caffeine inspiration, is the need to get away from the distractions that hound me at home and the office. I don't need perfect silence to write; I'm not a medieval monk working on an illuminated manuscript. I even welcome *some* distractions. The key for me is that they're not *my* distractions. So hearing the white noise of conversations or background music is fine. I hardly even notice *other* people's children wreaking havoc around me—I first started writing in coffee shops when my children were young and at home. As long as it's not *my* cell phone ringing or *my* children demanding my attention, all is well.

Research seems to support the fact that some people can concentrate better with background noise than absolute silence. A 2012 article in *The Journal of Consumer Research* shared results of a study conducted by researchers at the University of Illinois at Urbana-Champaign that had participants brainstorm ideas for new products while listening to various background noises at different volumes. They found that the level of noise in a typical coffee shop playing at about 70 decibels enhanced creativity and performance compared to the relative quiet of 50 decibels.[7]

The Thursday morning sermon-writing routine at
Redeye Roasters, overlooking Hingham Harbor.

Naturally an app was soon developed called Coffitivity that
allows people to work at home yet still enjoy the sounds of being in
a coffee shop. Or as they put it, "Coffitivity recreates the ambient
sounds of a cafe to boost your creativity and help you work better."
It's a free app, and you can try it out and decide for yourself, though
I'd prefer if it came with a downloadable cup of coffee.

Intersection of Coffeehouse and Church

Back in the 1990s, I tuned in regularly, if not religiously, to watch
NBC's smash sitcom *Friends*. Ross, Rachel, Chandler, Monica, and

Joey—they all sort of did become "friends" of mine. One of the things about these young urban professionals is they never displayed any sort of spiritual life. Maybe they were too busy or self-absorbed or the writers just didn't know how to work faith into the script. But they did have a central meeting place outside of their apartment that formed an integral piece of their communal identity: Central Perk, a coffee shop that appeared in nearly every episode and was the closest thing they had to a church.

Scholarly articles have been written about the coffee-shop boom that cite various factors for why the boom happened, including gentrification, the rise of Starbucks, technology driven by the internet, Wi-Fi, digital devices like laptops, and changing economic and employment conditions. I also think people crave community, and with the decline in religious affiliation, people seek places where they are known, welcomed, and comfortable.

Some coffee shops even appear to be out-churching churches. A powerful video was released several years ago titled "What if Starbucks Marketed Like the Church? A Parable." I often show it to people involved in newcomers ministries at my church because it highlights just how unwelcoming to visitors churches can be—and it's as frightening as it is revealing.

One of the most difficult things to do in life is to walk into a new church for the first time. Where do I park? Where's the entrance? Where do I go? Where do I sit? Can I safely leave my kids somewhere? Am I dressed appropriately? How much am I supposed to put into the collection plate? Will I be judged for saying the wrong thing? Not singing the hymns? Sitting when I'm supposed to kneel? Kneeling when I'm supposed to stand?

It's all bewildering, and this video exposes the many ways churches do this badly, from the confusing lingo to the locked doors to the unresponsive greeters. It's a hilarious parody that you should watch, but it's also a dark way of highlighting that many coffee shops do a better job welcoming people than churches. And that's pathetic.

Beyond the welcoming, many coffee shops do a better job advocating for environmental and economic justice than churches. We'll get into the whole Fair Trade, environmentally friendly conversation soon enough, but many coffee-shop owners are passionate about these issues in ways that put churchgoers to shame. I'm pretty sure Jesus himself would be drinking sustainable, organic, Fair Trade coffee had it existed in ancient Palestine. (As an aside, I find it remarkable he maintained his torrid pace of preaching, teaching, and healing without coffee. But then again, he did have that whole human/divine thing going, which must have helped.)

In churches, there's great rhetoric about following Jesus's teachings to help the poor, but a disconnect often exists between lofty ideals and action. When I served at a wealthy church in downtown Baltimore, I vividly remember preaching on the Parable of the Good Samaritan and then watching people leave church and walk right past a homeless man camped outside the front doors. This isn't an indictment of this particular community—I've done the same thing—and countless reasons exist to support organizations that help the homeless population rather than giving directly to individuals. But it was nevertheless disheartening.

At some urban coffee shops, owners and customers take matters into their own hands through what's become known as the "Pay It Forward" movement. The concept is simple and effective. When a customer buys a coffee, they have the option to pay in advance for someone else's cup—generally someone who couldn't otherwise afford it.

The idea actually goes back one hundred years to the working-class cafés in Naples, Italy, where the concept of *suspended coffee*, or *caffè sospeso*, first arose. It eventually became mostly a seasonal endeavor, and there is even a National Suspended Coffee Day in December. The idea went viral in 2013 when a plumber from Ireland started a Suspended Coffees page on Facebook. Now coffee shops all over the world participate in various ways—from chalk boards behind the counter to token systems.[8]

At its best, Suspended Coffee tangibly helps people in need. A free cup of coffee might not solve everyone's problems, but it can put a smile on someone's face and restore some dignity to a person whose dignity is regularly tested.

Colombian Vacation

You get some strange looks and comments when you tell people you're taking a family vacation to Colombia. "No," I felt the need to explain, "we're not going to Columbia, South Carolina. Or the District of Columbia. Yes, that's South America. No, I'm not too worried about getting kidnapped or becoming a drug lord and, while it would make for a fantastic church fundraiser, I don't intend on becoming a drug mule. I know you find this hard to believe, but I'm really more interested in the coffee than the cocaine."

Granted, Colombia *is* an unusual tourist destination for most Americans. But we decided to take a different sort of vacation a few summers ago, along with my brother and his three kids. We can't always get the five cousins together, but when we do, it's always a memorable experience for everyone.

My eldest and my brother's eldest are thirteen days apart (for nearly two glorious weeks I had the full attention of an extended family thrilled about the impending arrival of the first grandchild—until Matt made a similar announcement), and they both graduated from high school the same year. We decided to do something completely different for vacation since (1) this could be the last chance to have everyone together and (2) we're completely broke anyway now that we have to pay for college so why not go whole hog?

While Bryna and Matt were excited about the cross-cultural experience—the food, the nightlife, and exploring Cartagena's old walled city—and the younger kids were jazzed about the beaches and the older two were psyched about the prospect of legally drinking piña coladas, I was all about the coffee. Colombia is the world's third-largest coffee producer and the biggest producer of Arabica (the good ones!) beans.

When most people think of Colombian coffee, a single image comes to mind: Juan Valdez. This fictional coffee farmer was the 1958 creation of a Madison Avenue advertising firm contracted by the National Federation of Coffee Growers in Colombia. The purpose was simple—to create an image for coffee exclusively grown and harvested in Colombia, thereby setting it apart from other coffee-producing countries.

Juan Valdez soon became one of the most successful and identifiable brand images in the world. The white-hatted, poncho-wearing, mustachioed Valdez with his trusty mule at his side put Colombian coffee on the map. The television commercials asked, "Where do the beans come from?" And Juan Valdez would answer, strolling through lushly planted hills, "I handpicked them myself."

Of course, Juan Valdez also became mocked as a caricature and has been the target of countless internet memes. My friend Bob Weeks of Redeye Roasters, who once attended an international coffee festival in Colombia, calls him the "Ronald McDonald of the coffee world." As recently as 2009, the federation sued cartoonist Mike Peters, of *Mother Goose and Grimm* fame for a cartoon talking about Juan Valdez and Colombian coffee. Referencing violence in Colombia, he had a character say: "Y'know, there's a big crime syndicate in Colombia. So when they say there's a little bit of Juan Valdez in every can, maybe they're not kidding."

After years of conditioning, part of me assumed everyone I met in Colombia would sport a mustache, white hat, mule, and poncho. I was wrong. Colombia is a patchwork of cultures with a fascinating history and a rich blend of African, European, and indigenous influences.

With 2.2 million acres of Colombian highlands dedicated to coffee cultivation and over 500,000 individual family coffee growers (95 percent of whom farm fewer than five acres), the industry itself is ingrained in the national heritage. Colombians take tremendous pride in their global reputation for high-quality coffee beans. High altitude, rich volcanic soil, and predominantly shade-grown cultivation all contribute to a superior product. The rough, mountainous terrain also precludes mechanization, so the beans must all be hand-picked.

One of the sad realities of visiting coffee-producing nations, and Colombia is no exception, is most locals drink lousy coffee. It seems counterintuitive that a country harvesting some of the finest coffee on the planet would serve crappy coffee to the natives, but the good stuff gets exported at top dollar while the mediocre to middling stuff remains in country.

This is mostly an economic reality, but traveling to a coffee-producing Mecca and being served something you'd find at a Holiday Inn Express in Bayonne, New Jersey, is depressing. Fortunately, this culture is changing, or at least native specialty coffee shops that emphasize local coffee and seek to educate the population, are becoming more common.

In Cartagena, you can find some pretty lousy stuff that passes for coffee. It's sold on street corners and in restaurants and cafés all over town. But the good stuff is also available if you seek it out. One of my favorite finds was Café San Alberto, located on a side street near the Cartagena Cathedral called Calle Santos de Piedra. The coffee comes from the San Alberto farm in Buenavista in the Quindío region of Colombia, located in the central-western part of the country among the Andes Mountains.

The café is simple but well appointed, and the barista who served me was passionate about the coffee and genuinely excited to answer my questions about the farm and the family that has owned and operated it for generations. Plus, his name was Omar, which, if you remember your coffee history and the story of Omar the Dervish, is a fantastic name for anyone in the coffee business.

Another coffee shop I discovered was a newly opened café called Epoca Espresso Bar. I realize that's not the most Spanish-sounding name and they may be catering to Western tourists, but wow. I tasted several coffees, and the one that stood out was the San Donatto from

The barista at Epoca Espresso Bar in Cartagena, Colombia,
putting the finishing touches on my Chemex pour-over.

Colombia's Nariño region. Who doesn't like drinking fine coffee
named for a saint? Especially a fourth-century Italian saint who challenged and defeated a dragon by spitting on it after the dragon poisoned the local drinking well.

Two things stood out while spending time in such coffee shops: first, there's no hurry. You aren't there to just grab a to-go cup on your way to catch the commuter train. Artful coffee preparation takes time, whether it's served as an individual pour-over, out of a Chemex, or through a syphon. If you're in a rush, these shops will only frustrate you.

Second, the owners and baristas are proud of their product and seek to engage and educate their customers. Not everyone who works behind a counter at a coffee shop is interested in talking to you— maybe they're busy or cranky or in the midst of a double shift. Perhaps you're just dull. But if you ask about the coffee's origin or the barista's favorite roast and they light up, you can learn a tremendous amount about coffee and maybe even make a new friend.

Spending time over coffee—giving in to the process of precise preparation, lingering over the stunning aromas and hidden flavors—is an important spiritual discipline. Contrast this with the time most of us spend racing into coffee shops in America, grabbing a quick cup (extra shot!), and heading out the door. No, we don't always have time to linger over coffee—at times we treat it as little more than a caffeine transport system—but we need to make an effort to do just that, at least on occasion. It makes our entire lifelong coffee experience that much more fruitful and enjoyable.

Coffee's Shadow Side

The powers of a man's mind are directly proportioned to the quantity of coffee he drinks.

—Sir James Mackintosh, eighteenth-century
Scottish philosopher

A dark side hovers over coffee history that remains a bitter drink to swallow for people of faith: slavery. The legacy of enslavement goes hand-in-hand with the colonialism of the coffee trade, and we ignore it at our own peril, or at least our own ignorance. The slave trade followed the flag of empire, and the golden age of

European empire-building coincided with the rise of coffee culture on the continent.

The importation of black slave labor from Africa began with the Portuguese and Spanish, followed by the British, French, and Dutch. Sugar was the first major commodity to use slave labor and the plantation economy, with coffee following fast on its heels. Once coffee arrived, the soil of exploitation was already fertile—the slave trade was in place—and slavery extended easily enough to the mountainous coffee-growing regions.

First, it's helpful to learn how coffee, a plant indigenous to Ethiopia, even made it off the continent of Africa. In the early years of the coffee trade, Arab farmers and traders remained diligent about not allowing coffee plants to leave their native land. They recognized a good thing and did everything in their power to keep a firm grasp on their increasingly valuable cash crop.

Coffee Moves beyond the Muslim World

It wasn't until the seventeenth century that the early Arabian/African monopoly on coffee harvesting was broken. While growers sought to prevent the export of coffee plants, beans were a different story. But the beans were always parched, roasted, or boiled before leaving the country, so as infertile seeds they could not simply be planted, Jack-in-the-Beanstalk style.

It's said that a man named Baba Budan, an entrepreneurial-minded Sufi pilgrim from India who discovered the wonders of coffee at Mecca, smuggled seven fertile beans (seven being a sacred number in Islam) strapped to his stomach out of the Yemeni city of

Mocha. He successfully planted them in Chikmagalur (present-day Karnataka), a city in southern India, where the plants thrived.[1]

Naturally, an even more detailed story has been handed down as "Baba Budan and the Seven Seeds." During the seventeenth century, Baba Budan, a local holy man, rallied his fellow citizens in Chikmagalur to challenge an evil chieftain who had set up his murderous band in the Chandragiri Hills and wreaked havoc on the populace. Standing outside a holy cave, Baba Budan announced his intention to go on a pilgrimage to Mecca and suddenly disappeared into the cave. His faithful followers, both Hindu and Muslim, waited patiently outside the cave until Baba Budan reappeared.

Upon his return, he brought with him the miraculous news of a gift from the Holy Land, the seven seeds that would sustain them with food and drink. The coffee seeds were planted, and the Chandragiri Hills became known as the Baba Budan Hills. I'm not sure what happened to the malevolent chieftain, but by the time our hero returned to India, the threat was gone.

Baba Budan is still remembered and revered as something of a coffee savior. You can visit his grave located in India's Baba Budan Hills, and to this day numerous cafés and coffee blends bear his name all over the world from Edinburgh, Scotland, to Melbourne, Australia, to Cincinnati, Ohio.

Coffee and the Americas

Coffee made it to the Americas via an equally entertaining, if unlikely, tale. Louis XIV received a coffee plant as a gift from the Dutch, which was planted in the Jardin des Plantes in Paris. A French naval officer named Gabriel Mathieu de Clieu, who had been stationed in Martinique, was convinced coffee plants could thrive in Martinique, and after much court intrigue, the king's personal doctor secured him a cutting.[2]

In 1723, he set sail for Martinique with the rare coffee sprig encased in a glass chest, where he dutifully tended to it, sunning it up on deck each day and protecting it with his life. At various points, in no particular order, de Clieu fended off a fellow passenger who plotted to steal the plant and succeeded in shattering the glass case, the ship's crew fought off determined pirates in an all-day fight on the high seas, a massive storm arose and nearly destroyed the plant, and the supply of drinkable water onboard ran so low that de Clieu had to share his water rations with his prized possession.

In the end, de Clieu arrived on Martinique, battered plant in hand, and twenty months later he had his first harvest. Within a few years, coffee as a crop was thriving on Martinique, and the French king made him governor of the island. At least that's the swashbuckling tale, much of which is alleged to have been conveyed by de Clieu himself. Regardless, coffee made its way to the European colonies via the Atlantic Ocean and there it remains.

Slavery and Abolition

By 1750, coffee was being cultivated on five continents, and the growing and harvesting process of the coffee plant didn't happen by itself. It needed labor, and in order to quench the large and growing thirst for coffee it needed a lot of labor. To the detriment of humanity, much of that labor came over from Africa on slave ships.

As coffee lovers, it's exciting and romantic to think of the great eighteenth-century philosophers and thinkers drinking our favorite liquid in European cafés—the intellectual debate and witty repartee, new ideas fueling the Enlightenment. Voltaire (who reportedly drank forty to fifty cups a day), Immanuel Kant, Søren Kierkegaard, Denis Diderot, and others reflected, wrote, and conversed in coffeehouses.

Yet, all of this intellectual, coffee-inspired, groundbreaking work was, at one level, built on the back-breaking work of slaves who toiled in brutal conditions on coffee plantations. As one former slave of that era wrote of his French masters, "Have they not hung men with heads downward, drowned them in sacks, crucified them on planks, buried them alive, crushed them with mortars? Have they not forced them to eat shit?"[3]

By sheer volume, Brazil gets the prize for holding the most slaves in the Americas. The sugar trade served as coffee's dark forerunner, establishing the pattern of large-scale *fazendas* (plantations) run by the Portuguese in the seventeenth and eighteenth centuries. By the time coffee arrived, the ruthless system was already in place. Coffee was plugged in, and it quickly became the country's primary export. Interestingly, it was a Belgian monk who first planted coffee in the mountains of Rio de Janeiro in 1774. Little did he know the seeds he sowed would be reaped with songs of tears.

In time, two million slaves labored in Brazil, accounting for nearly one third of the country's population. The imported African slaves were regarded as subhuman, brutish animals to be abused, used, and discarded. Brazil was the last country in the world to abolish slavery, and only because they were pressured into giving up the lucrative trade by the rest of the world. As one member of the

Brazilian parliament, speaking for many, put it in 1880, "Brazil is coffee and coffee is the negro."[4]

In the nineteenth century, Britain played a major role in the drive to abolish slavery. They had the global standing and naval power to influence such a reversal, but mostly they had God on their side. Or at least they had a national come-to-Jesus moment through the writing, oratory, and passion of the Reverend William Wilberforce. After years of using the Bible and the notion of divine will to justify slavery, the eyes of Christians in Britain and elsewhere were suddenly opened to the folly of such a defense.[5]

Wilberforce, an evangelical Christian and member of Parliament, was instrumental in raising consciousness and highlighting the incompatible justification of slavery with the teachings of Jesus. The movement he spearheaded became what some might call the first grassroots human rights campaign. After raising awareness by graphically sharing the despicable reality of the slave trade, Wilberforce famously said, "You may choose to look the other way but you can never say again that you did not know." The tide turned and trafficking in human beings, which played a significant role in the rise of the global coffee industry, was no longer socially acceptable.

Economic Slavery

There may no longer be slavers full of Africans docking at ports in the Western Hemisphere, but economic slavery in the form of debt peonage continues in parts of the coffee-growing world. Many coffee-industry farm workers are effectively enslaved by large plantations through debt. When workers offer their labor in exchange for a loan, they enter a system of debt bondage where they lose control over their working conditions. Low wages, long hours, forced labor, and a lack of transportation all become a form of economic exploitation. The owners of these large plantations hold all the power in a system ripe for abuse. It's not slavery, per se, but there is often no way out and no means for recourse when ill-treatment occurs.

Where is this happening? A few years ago, the Brazilian government released its Dirty List of companies found to be holding people in "conditions analogous to slavery." This was defined as subjecting workers to "debilitating workdays, degrading conditions, debt bondage, and forced labor," all of which are illegal under Brazilian law. Fifteen coffee farms made the list.[6]

Seasonal workers sorting coffee at Finca Buena Vista in Nicaragua.

Catholic Relief Services' Coffeelands program looked into the list of fifteen and, while the means of exploitation varied, they found that in each case protective gear was not provided to workers while they applied toxic pesticides. They also found wretched, unsanitary living conditions, debt bondage, and the confiscation of IDs.

While these fifteen farms represent only a tiny fraction of the immense Brazilian coffee industry, such treatment is happening and cannot be ignored. It only underscores the importance for Global North coffee drinkers to keep asking questions about the sustainability of the coffee we drink.

Two of the largest coffee companies in the world, Nestlé (Nescafé, Nespresso, Taster's Choice) and Jacobs Douwe Egberts (huge in Europe), were forced to admit that beans from Brazilian plantations using slave labor ended up in their coffee. Despite corporate policies and ethical codes placed upon their suppliers, the companies claimed not to know the names of all the plantations that supply their beans. Again, asking questions is key—whether you're Nestlé or just someone who regularly drinks coffee.

Because the exploitation of fellow human beings continues, people of faith have a profound duty to address it. We may regret and repent of the harm done in the past, but the present is our responsibility to change.

Is Coffee a Sin?

As we've seen, coffee has not always had a trouble-free relationship with religious authorities. Muslims, Christians, and Jews have all engaged in their share of coffee battles. In some cases, this continues.

One of the few things outsiders know about the Church of Jesus Christ of Latter-Day Saints (LDS) is that caffeine is anathema. When Mitt Romney ran for president in 2012 as the first Mormon nominated by a major party, political observers were shocked that someone could mount a presidential campaign while not fueled by coffee. He lost, but still.

It's easy to assume this self-denial is a holier-than-thou thing, but the Book of Mormon itself says nothing about coffee. Followers of the LDS church believe in the concept of continuous revelation—that God continues to communicate with humans. In this light, founder and prophet Joseph Smith received a spontaneous manifestation of God's insight for living on February 27, 1833. This communication was written down, incorporated into the doctrine of the church, and is known as the Word of Wisdom. As part of the divine/human interaction, it's said that Smith asked for guidance on the matters of tobacco, warm drinks, strong drinks, wine, and assorted foods.[7]

The divine response to these questions included the directive that "hot drinks are not for the body or belly." As coffee and tea were the two popular "hot drinks" of the period, they were prohibited for observant Mormons.

Thus, caffeine itself is not banned but only coffee and tea. There has long been theological and moral debate over the consumption of caffeine-laden soft drinks. Mormon leadership has never officially taken a position on cola, but as recently as 1990 the church put out a statement advising "against the use of any drink containing harmful habit-forming drugs under circumstances that would result in acquiring the habit."[8]

Postum and the Rise of Mister Coffee Nerves

Many Mormons did find a coffee work-around. For generations they drank Postum—which was discontinued in 2007 (it reappeared in 2012 in limited locations, like Utah). Postum was introduced in 1895 by Post Cereal founder C. W. Post as a healthy alternative to coffee. Post was a Seventh-day Adventist opposed to coffee consumption and viewed caffeine as a culinary and moral evil, which is rich coming from the father of the company that brought us Fruity Pebbles cereal.

His advertising campaign for Postum meant to discredit coffee. With the vaguely threatening tagline There's a Reason, Post sought to highlight the alleged dangers of coffee. The hilarious cartoon devil-ghost Mister Coffee Nerves starred in Post's ads, hovering over cranky and sleepless coffee drinkers, before disappearing when they switched to Postum.[9] Postum became particularly popular during the coffee rationing of World War II, and became such a pervasive aspect of Mormon culture that families often referred to their home's coffee table as the "Postum table."

If you've never had the pleasure, Postum is a coffee- and caffeine-free roasted-grain beverage with molasses flavoring. Think instant coffee but without the caffeine. So basically, it's on Dante's ring-of-hell spectrum.

Caffeine Addiction

In the religious world, few stereotypes are as pervasive as an evangelical pastor hanging out in a local coffee shop, chatting people up, and posting pictures of a Bible verse next to his latte.

There's a whole hip pastor coffee schtick out there that gave me pause in even writing this book. As one clergy colleague said in the most sarcastic tone imaginable when I explained my latest writing project: "Coffee and faith? Oh, *that's* novel."

But still, if you dig deep enough into the evangelical movement, you can find pastors who are quick to find sin in the coffee-industrial complex. They won't condemn coffee, per se, as they'd alienate their entire flocks. They will, however, rebuke fellow Christians for falling into "caffeine addiction."

Obviously, coffee is not mentioned in the Bible, so pastors must take Scripture out of context by citing 1 Corinthians 6:12, a verse about sexual immorality, which says, "'All things are lawful for me,' but not all things are beneficial. 'All things are lawful for me,' but I will not be dominated by anything."

This passage often serves as the starting point to a discussion about caffeine addiction, something that can be railed against from the pulpit. Unless you're an avid coffee drinker, in which case there's the whole hypocritical, practice-what-you-preach thing.

While many of us joke about needing our next coffee "fix," the medical community doesn't see caffeine as an addiction issue as much as a dependence issue. Scientifically speaking, caffeine is not addictive. It *is* a stimulant that makes the user, er, consumer feel more alert and awake. Not that an actual coffee drinker needs medical research to prove this. Caffeine use does not, however, meet the National Institute on Drug Abuse's definition of addiction as "the uncontrolled use of a substance even when it causes negative consequences for the person using it." In other words, a regular coffee drinker who goes without it for a few days may experience headaches or irritability but will not engage in the self-destructive behavior of a drug addict.

The recently updated bible of the mental health profession, the *Diagnostic and Statistical Manual of Mental Disorders* (DSM-V), actually gave caffeine withdrawal its own entry, defined as "any withdrawal syndrome that occurs after abrupt cessation of caffeine intake." Common symptoms include "headache, anxiety, depression and low energy."[10] Because the withdrawal process is short and the symptoms are benign, formal treatment is not needed.

Too much caffeine can, however, have detrimental health effects, and, while there are no recorded cases of a coffee-deprived office worker holding up a local coffee shop and demanding an iced salted caramel latte, caffeine intoxication is another condition listed in the DSM-V, where it is defined as an "over-stimulation of the central nervous system caused by a high dose of caffeine." The DSM-V also cites coffee as "the most consumed psychoactive drug in the world," terming it "highly addictive" and noting it "can cause physical, mental, and psychomotor impairments." While coffee intoxication typically only lasts a day, the DSM-V alludes to the following symptoms: "restlessness, nervousness, excitement, insomnia, flushed face, diuresis, gastrointestinal disturbance, muscle twitching, rambling flow of thought and speech, tachycardia or cardiac arrhythmia, periods of high energy, or psychomotor agitation." None of which sounds like much fun.

In the end, it's worth noting that caffeine can indeed be lethal, though it would take herculean quantities. While researchers have proven that 1/67 of a gram of caffeine will kill a frog of moderate size, it would take significantly more to end a human life. There's a great online caffeine calculator that will tell you just how much caffeine would actually kill you. Enter your weight and drink of choice and voilà! In case you were wondering, 59.5 cups of coffee would do me in. Fortunately, I know a lot of clergy and would surely get a discount on the funeral costs.

Fair Trade, Fair Wage

That's something that annoys the hell out of me—I mean if somebody says the coffee's all ready and it isn't.

—J. D. Salinger, *The Catcher in the Rye*

When I first started drinking coffee, the major decisions I had to make were simple: (1) how much cream to add and (2) how much sugar to put in. I didn't think about what *kind* of coffee to use (whatever the church had on hand), and no one trusted me to brew it.

I arrived fresh out of seminary as the junior member of the clergy staff at Baltimore's Old St. Paul's Church, and found myself in the midst of an office coffee war. If the parish secretary made it to the kitchenette first, she brewed up a pot of weak coffee. If the head pastor got in early, he brewed it so strong you couldn't see light through the glass carafe. It was easy for me in my coffee naïveté. All I had to do was add more or less cream and sugar to make it bearable.

In those days, I certainly didn't consider where the coffee came from (a can), who grew it (some guy in Mexico?), or how it impacted the environment (obviously we'd toss the can into the office recycling bin). Years passed before I gave any thought to the people or issues behind the coffee. That only changed when I started frequenting an actual coffee shop run by knowledgeable and passionate coffee folks. Mike and Alicia at Coffee Labs cared not only about good coffee but also about the environment and conditions of farm workers. An activist's sense of social justice pervaded their shop. As a Christian minister, *I* should have been concerned with these issues, yet I'd never even given them fleeting consideration.

What I didn't recognize at the time was the fierce loyalty many independent coffee roasters have for the farmers who grow their coffee and their concern for the social and economic conditions of the pickers. There's a primary reason for this: they have relationships with them. Coffee is not just a product you get off the shelf at the grocery store or get served in a paper to-go cup. Coffee inspires human connection, and no one understands this better than the people who create such connections all over the world.

Fair Trade

Browsing the shelves at Coffee Labs, I noticed certain bags of coffee appeared to have recently returned from a Boy Scout Jamboree. They were emblazoned with all sorts of badges, in the form of stickers, touting things like Fair Trade and Shade Grown and Bird Friendly and Organic. I wondered what the bewildering array meant and why it even mattered.

Let's start with Fair Trade coffee. In theory, the idea is simple: pay a little more for your Fair Trade–certified coffee, and in exchange you receive peace of mind that the farmer who harvested it received a living wage amid good working conditions. The modern movement began in the 1940s as a few American and European relief organizations reached out to poor communities in Global South countries to help them sell their handmade products. Relieving the economic burden of exploited workers by providing a market where they could sell handicrafts at fair market prices was the goal. In time, Fair Trade certification, and the resulting sticker, became a signal to the consumer that the purchased product fairly compensated the producer. This movement quickly moved from handicrafts to spices, fruits, vegetables, sugar, honey, cocoa, rubber products, tea, and coffee.

Not surprisingly, the justice-driven Fair Trade movement claims religious roots. You may have shopped in a Ten Thousand Villages store and, if not, they're pretty fantastic. The concept, which offers consumers a place to purchase unique, fairly traded gifts, was pioneered by a Mennonite woman from Pennsylvania named Edna

Ruth Byler. Edna was a mother and an active member of the tight-knit Mennonite community in Akron known for her generous spirit and scrumptious cinnamon rolls.[1]

Her life changed after traveling to Puerto Rico with her husband in 1946, where she encountered a number of women in the La Plata valley struggling to feed their families. Struck by the beauty of their embroidery, Edna purchased a number of their wares to sell back home and return the money to the women in La Plata.

The relief organization of the Mennonite Church heard Byler's story, saw the potential impact of offering sustainable income opportunities for impoverished villagers, and soon began supporting her work on a larger scale, allowing her to travel to places like India and Jordan. By the 1950s, Byler was traveling the country in her Chevy with a trunk-load of global handicrafts, speaking to women's groups about the impact their purchases could make on the villages she visited. This humble and persevering Mennonite woman served as the inspiration behind Ten Thousand Villages and helped spur the global Fair Trade movement.

The promotion of Fair Trade for coffee didn't really take root until 1988, when a Dutch NGO, Solidaridad, working with small-scale Mexican coffee farmers, created the first Fair Trade certification initiative. This crusade succeeded, in large part, due to the passion of a Dutch worker-priest named Frans van der Hoff, who served in the slums of Mexico City before moving to rural southern Mexico. Moved by the economic plight of local coffee producers, van der Hoff helped farmers form a coffee cooperative in 1981 to bypass the local traders, derogatorily known as coyotes, who preyed upon the fiscal hardships of farmers.

From the modest initiatives of Solidaridad and TransFair International (founded in Germany in 1992, later rebranded as Fair Trade International), an international network of coffee Fair Traders was forged, with the intention of raising consciousness among consumers to the plight of small-scale coffee farmers.

The coordination of efforts culminated in 1997 with the formation of the umbrella group Fair Trade Labeling Organizations International (FLO-International). FLO sets the certification standards, conducts inspections, and supports disadvantaged growers. It also helps educate farmers on issues related to child labor (a practice that prevents certification), climate change, workers' rights, and gender equality.[2]

The system is predicated upon coffee growers paying a fee to FLO for the right to use the Fair Trade logo. The resulting certification provides consumers with assurance that the coffee they're purchasing meets Fair Trade criteria.

One of the things I love about the early Fair Trade coffee movement, besides the aspirations toward economic justice, is the name originally given to that first Dutch certification initiative. It was named Max Havelaar, after a fictional character in an 1860 novel by the Dutch author Eduard Douwes Dekker. In the book, *Max Havelaar: Or the Coffee Auctions of the Dutch Trading Company*, the protagonist battles against the corrupt and cruel government system in Java, which at the time was a Dutch colony.[3]

The book provoked so much controversy that Dekker, a former official of the Dutch East Indian Civil Service, published it under the pen name Multatuli. It focuses on the exploitation of the Indonesian coffee workers, and Max does all he can to protect the poor and bring justice to the powerless. In this rallying cry for those pushing for a moral economy, it is as inspiring as it is rare that this early Fair Trade organization was named after such a champion literary character.

At its best, Fair Trade coffee creates the perfect union between good coffee and economic justice. You can sip that coffee from Yemen with the knowledge that you are putting food on the table for a farmer and his family. It's coffee with conscience!

And yet, detractors criticize an imperfect system that often fails to live up to its lofty ideals. They point to unhappy farmers, lack of monitoring, bureaucratic red tape, corruption, and the cozy relationship between multinational corporations and the Fair Trade movement. A growing number of coffee-industry insiders believe the certification process is an empty one at best, a marketing ploy whose main goal is only to sell more coffee. At worst, it codifies exploitation and ignores human rights.

Indeed, the current Fair Trade marketplace reminds me of the boxing world. In the past, one single acknowledged and celebrated boxer, Rocky Marciano or Muhammad Ali or whoever, held the coveted title of Heavyweight Champion of the World. These days, it's unclear who gets called "Champ," as the balkanization of governing bodies (WBC, WBA, IBF, WBO, to name just a few) has muddied the pugilistic waters and created confusion for global boxing aficionados.

In the Fair Trade world, a similar plethora of certifications has arisen. Instead of being distinguished by gaudy bejeweled championship belts, the certifying organizations use different logos. There's Fairtrade International (FLO), the World Fair Trade Organization, Fair Trade Federation, and Fair TradeUSA, among others.

Corporations love the confusion because they can continue business as usual (maximize profits!), while selling some of their products under the label of a Fair Trade organization with lower standards. For many, it's little more than a promotional tool, allowing them to verbally support sustainability while monopolizing the landscape.

The Fair Trade movement continues to evolve as it confronts such challenges. Our global marketplace is certainly different from the era when Edna Byler drove around the country with her Chevy full of Puerto Rican textiles. The issues of economic independence and social justice and earning a living wage and seeking to get out of crippling poverty have not changed. We can and must act as consumers with a conscience if we hope to affect change.

Direct Trade

One way the specialty coffee industry has sought to help farmers while maintaining high quality is through direct trade with coffee growers. Direct trade allows roasters to form relationships with the farmers whose coffee they purchase, which eliminates the middlemen who take a significant cut in the supply chain. This puts more money directly into the farmer's pocket.

When I visited those coffee farms in Central America, I glimpsed the concept of direct trade firsthand. *Talking* about relationships is much less satisfying than *experiencing* relationships. Drinking beer with Mike, Dave, Francisco, Ronny, and Bram, after a full day of walking up and down steep hills in the mountains of Nicaragua—*that's* how relationships are forged. Swimming in a local Jinotega hot spring until midnight and being the only one sober enough to drive back to the hotel (ask me about dodging cows while driving a five-speed pickup truck full of coffee farmers down a winding mountain road) makes for a good story, but more importantly, it strengthens the bonds of friendship.

While Fair Trade has significantly improved the lives of many growers over the years, it does not account for quality—that's simply not the movement's focus, even if Fair Trade coffee does tend to taste better. For roasters who care about bringing quality coffee to their customers, direct trade means buying their coffee from farmers committed to growing outstanding coffee.

Direct trade allows roasters to find the best coffees, develop long-term relationships with the farms who grow them, and pay empowering wages to those involved in the agricultural process. Without articulated standards, the absence of accountability in the direct trade model makes some Fair Trade advocates nervous. In the end, many of the goals of Fair Trade and direct trade overlap: put more money into the pockets of farmers, end poor and hazardous environmental practices, and improve the lives of seasonal pickers and all those involved in bringing coffee to harvest. The methods differ and so does the end result, but it is heartening to learn that so many in the coffee industry seek to address prevailing inequities.

The Fair Trade movement has done great work in educating people on all ends of the coffee-producing and coffee-consuming spectrum on ways to alleviate poverty and maintain fairly sourced, sustainable coffee practices. Direct traders have built on much of this work and continue to push for better-quality coffee, which means higher prices and better environmental practices.

Equal Exchange

Some congregations attempt to bridge the coffee/social justice gap by intentionally serving ethically sourced coffee at all church functions. I met a group that refuses to leave this to chance. Though I had noticed the bright red bags of Equal Exchange coffee on the shelves of my local grocery store, I never paid them much attention. "That's nice," I thought to myself. "Do-gooders selling coffee. They're probably Unitarians."

What I didn't realize, until my friend Lane Lambert, a retired newspaper reporter and Equal Exchange coffee devotee, pointed out while drinking coffee with me one day at Redeye Roasters, was that their global headquarters and roastery is located a mere forty minutes away in West Bridgewater, Massachusetts. Naturally, I reached out to them, and they graciously invited me to stop by for a tour and some conversation.

Equal Exchange was founded in 1986 to challenge an existing model of global trade that favored large, multinational corporations at the expense of small farmers. They developed a model based on farmer cooperatives in producer nations that allows consumers with environmentally and economically based values to use their dollars in an empowering way. To differentiate themselves from the sometimes-co-opted global Fair Trade movement, Equal Exchange, which itself exists as a worker-owned cooperative, refers to their buying practices as "authentic Fair Trade" or "alternative Fair Trade." Navigating the complex waters of the modern Fair Trade movement, while keeping the needs of small farmers central to the mission, remains both the opportunity and challenge for this unique enterprise.

At the Equal Exchange roastery in West
Bridgewater, Massachusetts.

As for the coffee, Equal Exchange maintains an impressive roasting operation committed not only to the Fair Trade practices that
drive their core vision, but also quality. Ian McMillan, who over-
sees the co-op's coffee arm, told me they roast 7.5 million pounds
of coffee annually. That's a *lot* of coffee—nothing compared to the

88 million pounds roasted by Starbucks every year, but significantly more than the average independent coffee shop. Yet Equal Exchange isn't just hawking mediocre coffee, they stand firmly on the upper end of the quality spectrum, selling high-end coffees as single-origins and blends from all over the world.

At Equal Exchange, the connection between coffee and faith takes on tangible form. I spoke with three members of their inter-faith team, Peter Buck, Susan Sklar, and Bethany Karbowski, who highlighted Equal Exchange's partnerships with a broad array of denominational relief agencies. From Episcopal Relief & Development to Fair Trade Judaica to Catholic Relief Services, they recognize the buying power of faith-based consumers to make both a difference and a statement in the global marketplace.

At a micro level, Equal Exchange works with thousands of individual congregations to bring Fair Trade products to the post-worship fellowship hour. In addition to coffee, which makes up 70 percent of the business, Equal Exchange offers a variety of Fairly Traded products like chocolate, tea, and even bananas and avocados. In effect, each congregation becomes a mini, weekly, hour-long Equal Exchange Café, offering delicious coffee while subtly educating parishioners about the importance of respecting the dignity of global food producers.

I love the concept of connecting socially conscious consumers to products that have been fully vetted and deemed socially responsible. Over a nice, balanced cup of Peruvian coffee, Susan Sklar, who is married to Rink Dickinson, one of Equal Exchange's cofounders, spoke of "mission match" between the Equal Exchange model and the faith-based community. This resonated with me because if there's anything that transcends denominational boundaries, it should be helping people in the Global South receive fair wages.

People so often lament the inability to make a difference in the world. The problems that bombard us through the daily news cycle feel insurmountable. Between natural disasters and violent crime and crippling poverty, we all want to "do something," yet feel paralyzed by the insignificance of our local contribution to global tribulations. It never feels like enough, so we turn up the volume on our lives, reenter the bubble in which we exist, and bury ourselves in the minutiae of life.

The Equal Exchange concept reminds us that small things make a difference, that tiny acts of faith and service and kindness matter. Because, echoing Jesus's words in Matthew 25:40, "Just as you did it to one of the least of these . . . you did it to me," seeing Christ in one another is a hallmark of the Christian faith.

Jesus reminds us again and again that small things, like purchasing a bag of coffee that benefits female farmers in the Congo, are just as important as grand gestures. It's why he tells his disciples that faith the size of a mustard seed can move mountains; praises the lone leper who returned, after being healed, to say "thank you"; and washes feet and cooks breakfast and interacts with children. Small gestures point to a big heart, serving as windows into our souls while offering hope to a broken world.

Few of us will become spiritual heroes like Gandhi or Desmond Tutu or Mother Teresa or the Dalai Lama. But collectively, many people doing small acts can become a movement—and that's the spirit that pervades Equal Exchange.

Coffee Activism?

Full disclosure: I'm not an activist. I follow Jesus, who challenged his disciples to take up their crosses and follow him, but I'm not one to pick up a placard and wave it around city hall. I support those who do, hopefully even inspiring others through my preaching and writing, but I'm more apt to post to Twitter about an issue of social justice or preach about it than march in the streets. I'm not necessarily proud of this, but I take solace in the fact that, as Saint Paul puts it, "there are varieties of gifts" (1 Corinthians 12:4) and that, "the gifts [Jesus] gave were that some would be apostles, some prophets, some evangelists, some pastors and teachers, to equip the saints for the work of ministry" (Ephesians 4:11–12a). In other words, among the worshipping community, all the skills exist, but no single person has a monopoly on them. I find this liberating, as it eases the pressure to be all things to all people.

My outlook on personal activism changed slightly, however, after I received an invitation to attend an Equal Exchange Action Forum. With the tagline Learning Together—Sharing Together—Building a Movement Together, this was an opportunity to gather with the worker-owners of the Equal Exchange cooperative and fellow consumer-activists to help shape the future of the alternative Fair Trade movement. I learned a ton, met some passionate people, and realized coffee was my gateway drug to community activism.

It's one thing to meet some coffee farmers and have your eyes opened to the inequities of globalization. The next step is finding practical ways to alleviate the issues of poverty through informed consumer choices. Partnering with a unique organization like Equal Exchange and purchasing their products means supporting small farmers. It's as simple as that.

In an era of hyper-intense consolidation in the food industry in general, and the coffee industry in particular, small farmers continue to get squeezed. This is intuitive when you consider how corporations now own the vast majority of the coffee market. Corporations care primarily about profit, not people. This isn't to trash everyone who works for corporate America or to label corporations as evil, rather it speaks to the hard truth spelled out by economist Milton Friedman, who declared, "The social responsibility of business is to increase its profits."[4]

Fortunately, for ethically minded consumers who value humanity over revenue yet still crave quality coffee, another way exists. The wider Equal Exchange community is a place where a passion for coffee and social justice merges to create conscious consumers. For me, and I hope for you as well, *that's* worth fighting for. Look for my newfound activism as I work to encourage all congregations, starting with my own, to serve only fairly traded coffee at all future church events. That seems like low-hanging coffee activism fruit.

Goodbye Styrofoam: Environmental Impact

Coffee first. Save the world later.

—Caroline George, *The Vestige*

If you ever need a firsthand account that climate change is real, speak with a coffee farmer. When I was in Nicaragua, the exporter I met, Francisco, was frustrated because he kept getting coffee orders he couldn't fill. Production was down by nearly 40 percent from previous years. Customers were demanding coffee he simply could not provide, and he was very clear about the reason: global warming.

This is a familiar story in nearly every coffee-producing region on the planet. Increased periods of drought, higher temperatures, plant disease (including the dreaded leaf rust), and the killing off of insects that pollinate coffee plants—all associated with climate change—have been linked to decreased production. The microclimates where some of the best coffee grows remain particularly sensitive to even small increases in temperature. A recent study focused on Ethiopia predicted that up to half the country's coffee-growing regions may not survive global warming, likening this to France losing one of its great wine regions.[1] Another concluded that about half the acreage currently producing specialty coffee would be unproductive by 2050.[2]

One solution for farmers is to move their production to higher elevations where temperatures are cooler. It doesn't take a geologist to realize, however, that there's only so much mountain. This also makes transporting coffee down the mountain that much more difficult, not to mention the three to four years it takes for a new coffee plant to start producing a significant yield.

Farmers across the "bean belt" are getting nervous, and consumers should be as well. In addition to the reduction in areas suitable to farming, some producers are turning to the more disease-resistant Robusta plants (that's the coffee that tastes like burnt rubber) rather than Arabica.

Coffee agronomists continue to experiment with disease- and weather-resistant hybrids and adaptive plants while seeking to maintain flavor, but results are slow. Between keeping these folks in your prayers and making ethically based consumer choices, we can all pitch in by reducing our own carbon emissions footprint. Putting solar panels on your house, composting coffee grounds, or biking to work or church is a small price to contribute to coffee's future. Plus, it would be a shame if coffee became a luxury item for the wealthy rather than a staple enjoyed across the wide swath of humanity.

Shade Grown

Back to the coffee-bag stickers. Another sticker you see on some specialty brands announces that the coffee is "shade grown." Shade grown is all about ecological impact, and it's gotten a lot of press in recent years. There are two distinctive stickers to look for. One has a bunch of birds on a green background with the words "bird friendly." The other has a green frog with "Rainforest Alliance" on the label. These certifications, supplied by the Smithsonian Migratory Bird Center and Rainforest Alliance, respectively, mean that a biologist has surveyed the farm to confirm it meets criteria related to tree diversity, pesticide use, and sustainable soil.

For generations, shade-grown coffee, cultivated under canopies of larger trees, was how small-scale farmers grew and tended their beans, and many still do. Standing next to coffee plants under the cover of shade trees at Finca El Paraiso in El Salvador was a beautiful sight to behold. I also learned that native shade trees such as banana, orange, and lemon positively impact the flavor in the cup by adding nitrogen balance to the soil.

In the 1970s, a strain of sun-tolerant coffee plants was developed, and this, coupled with mechanization, allowed large-scale coffee producers to clear-cut huge areas and engage in open-planting. While this greatly increased the growers' yield, it had a negative impact on

Under the tropical canopy of shade-grown coffee trees.

the environment. In particular, millions of acres of rainforest were destroyed in the name of profit (shocking, I know). Strip away the forest-like nature of coffee farms, which provide a natural habitat for migratory birds, butterflies, bats, ants, small reptiles, and fauna, and it doesn't take Henry David Thoreau to figure out bad things will happen to the environment.

Basically, full-sun coffee farms are the puppy mills of the coffee industry. The two worst offenders are the world's two largest coffee-producing nations, Brazil and Vietnam, where up to 75 percent of coffee production takes place without the cover of trees. These lower-quality full-sun coffees, usually the Robusta variety, typically end up in instant coffees and supermarket big cans.

As with all things coffee, just because it's shade grown doesn't necessarily mean the final product tastes better. It *usually* does, but some fantastic non-shade-grown coffees exist because high altitudes preclude shade trees (hello, Kenya!). The rich, biodiverse soil of shade-grown coffee makes a big difference in the flavor, but other factors also contribute. Besides altitude, when it comes to brewing a top-notch cup of coffee, soil quality, harvest and processing techniques, roasting, water condition, and brewing method all impact the final flavor.

Shade-grown, bird-friendly coffee is definitely a good thing, especially when the other option is purchasing mass-produced, mechanized beans. But when it comes to taste, sometimes it's just nice to imagine exotic birds flying overhead as your coffee is being hand-picked by a coffee farmer earning a fair wage.

Organic

In the United States, coffee producers can only receive the organic seal (another sticker!) if they refrain from using pesticides, herbicides, fungicides, or fertilizers. It's not as if these chemicals affect the final product. When you're sipping a cup of conventional (i.e., nonorganic) coffee, you won't sit around saying, "I taste a few floral notes, perhaps some vanilla, and just a hint of DDT." These get washed off or burned away before entering your cup. The greatest impact of synthetic pesticides is twofold: environmental and worker health.

The environmental factor relates to the shade-grown issues—without tree cover and the natural fertilizer of these mini-ecosystems, farmers must rely on chemical pesticides. When it rains, soil is washed away along with the natural nutrients, which in time makes the soil un-tillable. The rainwater carries away not only the nutrients but the chemicals, which end up in the local water supply.

The other main issue is worker health. Farmers exposed to high levels of toxic chemicals while spraying or harvesting crops incur health hazards that put workers and entire villages at risk for disease and premature death.

Not every organically grown coffee automatically carries the organic label, however. Many small coffee farms have been organic operations for generations but are unwilling or unable to pay for the certification process. Thus their coffees don't carry the official sticker even though they qualify. This remains another example of why it's helpful to know the farms, or at least go to coffee shops where the owners know the farms. Obviously, that can of Maxwell House won't be organic coffee, but that small bag you pick up from your favorite specialty shop may well be, even if it isn't labeled as such.

K-Cups

People sure love their Keurig machines. By some accounts, Keurig Green Mountain sells over nine billion K-Cups annually.

When Keurig's single-cup brewing system was introduced in the 1990s, many coffee-drinking households rejoiced. You want a cup of medium roast coffee? Your wife wants a cup of decaf? Your surly teenager wants a bold French roast to propel her onto the early morning school bus? No need to brew three pots of coffee. Just grab three plastic pods and voilà! Everybody's happy!

We saw a coffee-brewing revolution happening right before our eyes. In the early days, Bryna and I got swept up in this and even ordered one. We tried the coffee a few times but between the pre-ground coffee and the inability to control brew strength (each pod contains 11 grams of coffee), we returned it a week later and stuck to our drip-coffee guns.

For the past decade, there has been growing concern about the single-cup brewer's environmental impact. In early 2015, a Canadian video production company released a two-and-a-half-minute mock horror film turned viral video called "Kill the K-Cup." Featuring a Godzilla-like creature made entirely of K-Cups, explosions, city dwellers fleeing in terror, and Star Wars-esque fighter planes comprised of K-Cups, the hellfire and brimstone video was intended to make a bold statement about the environmental impact of the billions of plastic pods ending up in landfills.

This isn't to shame anyone who brews with K-Cups. Some of my best friends swear by them (looking at you, Hans). But it's important to be aware of the environmental impact of convenience. Keurig Green Mountain insists they are continuing to develop fully recyclable pods, and Nespresso's single-cup brewer uses aluminum pods.

Still, as the "Kill the K-Cup" video highlights, in 2014 enough K-Cups were sold that, if placed end-to-end they would circumnavigate the globe over ten times. John Sylvan, who invented the Keurig machine as a twentysomething living in Boston and sold it to Green Mountain Coffee in 1997, has publicly expressed remorse for having invented it. He's even started a company that sells solar panels, in part, I presume, to atone for the environmental issues he helped spawn.

He also knew his Keurig (which means "excellence" in Dutch) pods would sell, and he's made a lot of money on the concept. As he puts it in retrospect, "It's like a cigarette for coffee, a single-serve delivery mechanism for an addictive substance."[3]

Despite the publicity around the alleged environmental disaster that is the K-Cup, single-pod coffee brewers continue to thrive. Some predicted doom for Keurig Green Mountain when the K-Cup patent ran out in September of 2012, but the consumer appetite has only increased.

I recently went for a stroll around Bed Bath & Beyond (yes, it was under duress; no, I'm not a regular customer) and was stunned by the number of different companies selling coffee pods. From Starbucks to Dunkin' Donuts to Newman's Own to McCafé and everything in between, it was like entering a pod-people emporium. There was even a Margaritaville coffee pod display with the tagline, "A Taste of Paradise." Now, I'm a big Jimmy Buffet fan. And I'm a big coffee fan. But nobody needs coffee from Jimmy Buffett.

What's in Your Mug?

In the end, coffee, like many things in life, can both help and hurt people and the environment. When coffee is cultivated with traditional, shade-grown methods, it can help preserve and protect valuable natural habitats. It can provide good work for people in rural villages where few other options in poor, coffee-producing regions are available. Yet, coffee can also result in actions that poison the environment and destroy the health of workers who earn little more than slave wages. As consumers, we have a choice of which type of coffee culture we want to support.

There are market forces and international situations that make all of this complex. I'm not going to reduce the ethical considerations to a simplistic "What Would Jesus Brew?" (Though I could probably make a killing selling WWJB bracelets.)

For me, much of this has to do with simple awareness when having my morning coffee. Can I really afford, spiritually speaking, to ignore the conditions in which my favorite beverage made it to my mug? Morally and ethically, I'm no longer comfortable with a "don't ask, don't tell" policy.

In the cycle of confession and repentance that is an integral part of all faiths, I find two petitions in the Ash Wednesday liturgy particularly instructive when it comes to my relationship with coffee. This is the day that Christians begin the season of Lent, and there is a long Litany of Penitence in the Episcopal tradition that includes asking God to "accept our repentance for the wrongs we have done: for our blindness to human need and suffering, and our indifference to injustice and cruelty" and confessing "our waste and pollution of your creation, and our lack of concern for those who come after us."

I find these powerful reminders to be mindful of the many ways, both known and unknown, that we are blind to injustice and to the self-centeredness that drives so many of our decisions. We may not be able to change the past, but we can and should ask questions before making our present choices. I know I strive to do so, and I invite you to go and do likewise.

Church Coffee: A Mixed Blessing

We ought therefore to show hospitality . . . so that we may work together for the truth.

—3 John 8 NIV

Few things unite worship experiences across denominations and faiths like the post-liturgy coffee hour. This "liturgy" following the liturgy adds an essential exercise in building community. In most congregations, during the worship itself people sit in pews or chairs facing the front. It's understandable as that's where the action is. Whether it's the preacher nattering on or the choir singing or ritual sacramental action, it happens up front for all to see. People pray and sing and nod at one another, but worship isn't conducive to a full-on conversation about the Cubs or a theological debate over the sermon or comforting a friend during a particularly trying time.

That's the purpose of coffee hour. It is the time when people gather to do what communities do: laugh, comfort, debate, chase children around, and share pictures of grandchildren. It's intergenerational in a world that lacks connection between the generations; it's face-to-face in a society that avoids contact beyond video screens; it breaks down barriers between people who have disparate worldviews, occupations, and concerns but share a common religious faith and identity.

We joke about coffee being the eighth sacrament (or third if you're Protestant), but truth abounds. If a sacrament is an outward and visible sign of an inward and spiritual grace, coffee fits the description. It binds communities together in ways that books, even the most sacred books, sometimes fail to do, because coffee fosters relationship. And relationship—with the divine and one another—is the bedrock of a faith community.

Coffee Hour

Some of my earliest church memories revolve around coffee hour, and this did much to cement my budding relationship with faith. As a youngster, I sang in the boys' choir at St. David's Episcopal

Church in Baltimore's Roland Park neighborhood. This was serious stuff, with rehearsals three times a week plus Sundays, and, as we got paid a stipend, I consider it my first job. Something had to pay for all those packs of baseball cards!

My best friend Ned and I had no interest in the post-service coffee. But we found our own personal metaphor for the kingdom of Heaven inside a small, china bowl dutifully set out each Sunday by the well-coiffed coffee-hour ladies: sugar cubes. We devised a variety of subversive tactics for raiding the bowl without notice and then sharing the sugary bounty with one another.

In retrospect, I can't imagine our subterfuge went unnoticed, but this speaks more to the communal nature of coffee hour than any elementary-school-aged Sunday morning sugar high. Coffee hour provided a comfortable bubble in which children could bond while adults conversed, even while testing the limits of independence. I may not recall any sermons from my years as a choirboy, but I do fondly remember those coffee-hour sugar cubes and the joy of church as a second home.

Today's coffee-hour experience hearkens back to the coffeehouses of yore. No one sits in a corner pounding on their laptop demanding the Wi-Fi password (which I'm always happy to give out, by the way). No, they're . . . wait for it . . . engaging with other people! Perhaps gossiping about the pastor's recycled sermon or making plans to start a new church committee, but whatever the topic of conversation, it's sure to be lively.

For visitors, however, coffee hour can be intimidating. Walking into a party where everyone seems to already know one another is an introvert's nightmare. I've visited churches where I've literally stood around awkwardly waiting for someone to acknowledge my presence before slinking out the side door when no one even bothered to say hello.

At one level, I get it. People who genuinely enjoy one another yet only see each other once a week want to connect. That's one of the great joys of coffee hour—connecting with friends you don't get to see every day. In a very real way, fellow congregants are part of an extended family, and coffee hour can feel like a weekly family reunion.

Yet I worry when people insist on referring to their faith community as a *family*. There are surely aspects of that, but I think they have an idealized Norman Rockwell vision of family life. We may fully be our authentic selves in a family setting, but families are also dysfunctional, closed groups. You are either in or out. For those seeking a church home, entering coffee hour can feel like intruding on a family gathering already in progress. And who wants to go to someone else's Thanksgiving dinner where you don't know anyone and have to suffer through someone *else's* drunk uncle's unenlightened political commentary?

The notion of Christian hospitality can play a vital role here. Jesus spent a lifetime breaking down barriers between and among people, most especially in social settings around food and drink. There must be an element of invitation in our post-worship coffee hours, of welcoming the stranger, of reaching out to those on the margins. Being aware of those dancing along the fringes and drawing them in is a vital aspect of healthy community, the responsibility not just of the pastor but of each congregation member. I always encourage my parishioners to enjoy one another's company at coffee hour but to remain cognizant of those existing on the sidelines and to be vigilant in welcoming strangers.

One hopefully nonthreatening way we do this at St. John's is setting aside special mugs for visitors and newcomers. On the large table where the coffee is set up, we place a number of large green mugs, which contrast with the hordes of ordinary white ones. We encourage visitors to use green mugs for their coffee (or tea, if they insist) as a sign that they are new and open to conversation. In a fairly large church, it's not always evident who is new. Who among us *hasn't* mistakenly welcomed someone who has then turned around and indignantly replied they've been going to this church for thirty-three years, thank you very much? Oops. It's enough to make anyone a bit gun-shy in the welcoming department.

The green mugs work because they give the newcomer the control. No one compels them to take one if they'd rather fly under the coffee-hour radar, and using one also doesn't automatically trigger a spontaneous group hug. Though for some reason, our Newcomer's Committee didn't like my idea of offering mugs with giant red targets on them.

Church Coffee

Churches are notorious for serving bad coffee. You know, the Folgers brewed in huge metal urns from the 1970s served in Styrofoam cups in a dimly lit church basement. After an inspiring worship service in which we offer God our very best efforts of devotional practice, how dispiriting to then invite parishioners and visitors into the spiritual equivalent of a buzz kill.

"We've glorified God through fancy vestments, celebrated communion with silver chalices, preached and prayed with every ounce of our being. Now here's some crappy coffee to complete the tableau." An obvious disconnect exists between what we *proclaim* with our lips and what we then *bring* to our lips.

But it doesn't have to be this way. With a little effort and a slight increase in expense, worshipping communities can easily up their fellowship game. Because while this is partly about the coffee, it's mostly about the community.

I'm convinced that when people drink good coffee they tend to linger after church and engage in deeper conversation. And when people stay longer and converse more, the bonds of community are strengthened. I'm not saying that Jesus's original disciples formed a glorified coffee klatch, but just as Jesus continually drew people into community, coffee can help do the same.

So being mindful of what you serve at coffee hour is really an investment in community. Sure, I'd personally love it if someone would donate an $8,000 industrial-grade espresso machine to my parish (I'll put your name on a brass plaque!). But just taking the time to provide decent, fairly traded coffee is both a social and social-justice upgrade.

Coffee Hour Gone Wrong

Occasionally it's not just bad coffee that ruins the coffee hour vibe. In April of 2003 in the town of New Sweden, Maine (population 651), someone laced the post-church coffee at Gustaf Adolph Lutheran

Church with arsenic. A seventy-eight-year-old parishioner died, and fifteen other mostly elderly parishioners became seriously ill.[1]

Like something out of *Murder, She Wrote*, the story caught the attention of the national news media and briefly shoved this tiny town in rural northeast Maine into the spotlight. The following month, a fifty-three-year-old man, identified as the primary suspect in the poisoning, died of a self-inflicted gunshot wound at his farmhouse. In a suicide note, Daniel Bondeson confessed to putting liquid arsenic in the coffee urn, indicated that he acted alone, but provided no motive.

The small church, built by Swedish settlers and named after a seventeenth-century Swedish king, had no permanent pastor at the time. Adding to the intrigue, many survivors don't blame Bondeson for the poisoning, which was investigated by local police as well as the FBI.

On the other hand, Bondeson's suicide note seems pretty clear: "I acted alone. I acted alone. One dumb poor judgement ruins life but I did wrong." He did indicate that while he attempted to make his fellow parishioners sick, he didn't realize the chemical he put into the coffee was poison. "I thought it was something? I had no intent to hurt this way. Just to upset stomach, like the churchgoers did me."[2] Apparently Bondeson was angry with church leadership over a new communion table he donated to the church in memory of his late mother and father.

What's so shocking about this incident, besides murder, is the shattering of the sanctity of coffee hour. When we think about it, few places feel so safe. Children play, people converse, thoughts are shared, coffee is imbibed, and usually no one is poisoned.

Monastery Visit

Monks make many things. From ale to cheese to fruitcake, monasteries churn out some amazing, artisanal foodstuffs in addition to illuminated manuscripts and chanted psalms. When I discovered that the monks at the Monastery of St. Tikhon of Zadonsk in Waymart, Pennsylvania, were roasting coffee along with their daily prayers, I made a pilgrimage to meet these holy men.

St. Tikhon's, founded in 1905 and nestled amid the Poconos, is the oldest monastery of the Orthodox Church in America, an Eastern Orthodox Church with Russian roots. I reached out to the monks to ask if I might join them for a couple days after Easter to worship with them and meet the monks who roast the coffee. They were very open to the idea, and when the time came, I eagerly hopped in my car for the five-hour drive to northeast Pennsylvania.

The opportunity to learn more about the Orthodox Church beckoned as a side benefit to the trip, beyond the coffee. As a Westerner, Eastern Orthodoxy has always seemed shrouded in mystery, clouds of incense, and long beards. In order to blend in, I kept my scraggly and shockingly gray sabbatical facial hair going. The gracious monks, from the abbot, Father Sergius, down to the novices, welcomed me as "Father Timothy," a brother in Christ.

The liturgies I attended, which take place at 6:00 a.m. (before coffee!) and 4:30 p.m., averaged two hours in length with lots of standing. In my own Anglican tradition, that's as long as any service we hold. Ever. Our Easter Vigil, the holiest service of the year, *might* be two hours, and people still complain it's too long. For the monks at St. Tikhon's, a two-hour liturgy is simply called "Wednesday." After two hours, they're just getting warmed up.

As I told several of the brothers, the Orthodox must have the strongest calves in all of Christendom. My feet were burning as I listened to divine harmonies, gazed upon beautiful icons, inhaled fragrant incense, and witnessed some of the oldest Christian liturgies, including the Divine Liturgy of St. John Chrysostom, which dates to the fourth century.

These monks also adore their coffee. My first morning at the monastery, after surviving the early service, I joined the brothers for breakfast in their dining room, where a stunning mural-like icon of the last judgment covers one entire wall. One of the brothers, originally from Ukraine, brewed some delicious coffee from Rwanda roasted by a fellow monk. Brother Paul told me that he and several of the brothers actually prefer Turkish coffee and showed me the copper *ibrik* they use to make it. For him, it's an afternoon delight rather than a morning brew.

If you've never had Turkish coffee, it's worth trying, as it's the preferred brewing method in many parts of the Arab world and Eastern Europe. I first sampled it when I traveled to Jordan, in the Middle East, a few years ago. Basically, it's a filterless method of brewing finely ground coffee over a gas stove. It is strong, sludge-like, and an acquired taste. It made sense that coffee-loving monks with Russian roots would have some Turkish coffee aficionados among their ranks. Before leaving the monastery, Brother Paul insisted on making me a cup from his stash of imported Turkish coffee—a tiny cup, actually, as it's served in a demitasse. Good stuff.

The idea to start roasting coffee at the monastery happened organically. The monks were already running the country's largest Orthodox bookstore, fueled in part by St. Tikhon's Orthodox Theological Seminary, located across the street from the monastery.

In front of the roaster at St. Tikhon's Monastery
with Father Innocent and Brother Stephen,
under the watchful eye of their patron.

In 2016 the monks added coffee roasting to the mix, with the roaster itself set up inside the bookstore. In many ways, the place feels like any bookstore/café except the roasters and baristas all wear cassocks and sport ZZ Top-like beards instead of skinny jeans and nose rings.

One of my favorite aspects of the monks' roasting operation is the name of the coffee itself. They market and sell specialty ethically sourced beans from around the world as Burning Bush Coffee. There's an obvious connection to the story of Moses and the burning bush in Exodus, but in Orthodox theology another layer of meaning exists. In the Eastern Church, they understand the flame Moses perceived as God's Uncreated Energies/Glory. This event transcends stand-alone miracle and gains significance as an episode that prefigures the virgin birth of Jesus. Mary as the *Theotokos* (God-bearer) giving birth without losing her virginity parallels the bush being burned but not consumed. Regardless of where you stand on the doctrine of the Virgin Birth, using coffee to highlight a fine point of theological conviction is high-level evangelism.

To further the point, every bag of coffee roasted at St. Tikhon's includes a quote from Saint Gregory of Palamas. "The world is a burning bush of God's energies," proclaims the fourteenth-century theologian and archbishop of Thessaloniki. So much better than "the best part of waking up is Folgers in your cup."

I sat down with Father Innocent over a delightful and flavorful cup of organic Ethiopian coffee from the Guji Alaka region. Father Innocent is not one of the monks—he's a local Orthodox priest—but he manages the bookstore and played an integral role in bringing the monastery into the coffee business. Father Innocent is as passionate about roasting coffee and bringing out the flavor of each bean as he is about his faith, and it shows in the coffee.

These monks aren't roasting coffee as a gimmick. Rather, just as they give their best to God through worship, at Father Innocent's insistence they seek to roast the best possible coffee. The coffee, sold to individual customers as well as churches all over the world through St. Tikhon's website, has been a successful venture.

It helps that the monks view their foray into coffee as an act of local hospitality. They sell cups of incredible coffee for $1 a cup. When I visited, you could choose between coffee from Ethiopia, Rwanda, Costa Rica, or their popular Monastery Blend. The comfortable leather couches, impressive array of books, and free Wi-Fi added to the ambience.

Father Innocent told me about a young woman who lives nearby who frequents the bookstore because she loves specialty coffee. Until Burning Bush Coffee arrived, she had never stepped foot onto the monastery grounds, despite having lived in the area her whole life. Suddenly, she was conversing and making friends with bearded monks with whom her path never would have crossed.

At St. Tikhon's the monks have harnessed the potential power of coffee to break down barriers between people. They aren't actively proselytizing when people wander in—visitors are handed coffee, not tracts. Perhaps this young woman has no interest in religion, and that's fine. Yet the monks are now part of her world, and who knows what God might do with that relationship one day?

My last afternoon at the monastery, I hung out with Brother Stephen as he fired up the roaster with ten pounds of coffee from Ethiopia. As he dutifully kept his eye on the gauge displaying the internal temperature of the beans, he patiently endured my flurry of questions about roasting coffee along with a few on the finer points of Orthodox liturgy. The aroma of roasted coffee filled the air, and Brother Stephen reminded me that the Ethiopian Orthodox Church had banned coffee until 1889, erroneously viewing what is now the country's national drink as a threat to Christianity. Afterward, he presented me with a bag of the coffee he had just roasted, another indication of the monks' inspiring hospitality and generosity.

Before departing St. Tikhon's, I tracked down Father Innocent for a final query. I had been waiting months to ask this holy roaster if he found roasting coffee to be a spiritual exercise. I envisioned some profound answer, dripping with theology and the meaning of life.

Father Innocent told me that for him roasting is sometimes meditative and sometimes chaotic. At times the rhythm of the roast takes hold and it becomes like a dance between the beans and the fire. At other times, it's less contemplation and more freaking out trying not to burn the beans.

I loved this answer, rather than my idealized imagined one, because it reflects an authentic experience of the life of faith. Sometimes everything falls into place and great harmony exists with God, with the universe, with our selves. And sometimes the chaos of life keeps the divine hand hidden from our eyes. I guess that's why you spend time with coffee-roasting monks—you come for the coffee and stay for the wisdom.

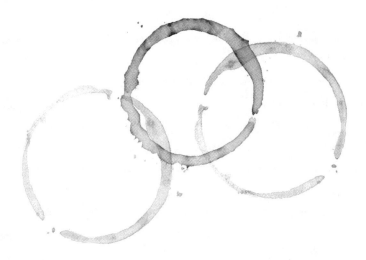

Last Sip

As soon as coffee is in your stomach, there is a general commotion. Ideas begin to move . . . similes arise, the paper is covered. Coffee is your ally and writing ceases to be a struggle.

—Honoré de Balzac, nineteenth-century French novelist

Thank you for joining me on this caffeinated journey of discovery. I hope you learned a few things, reveled in the stories of faith that comprise the history of this beautiful beverage, enjoyed meeting some folks behind the global coffee industry, smiled a bit, and shared in a deeper sense of our spiritual interconnectedness.

Like faith, coffee straddles both the individual and communal aspects of our lives. We all have personal preferences, but they are often best shared in community. At its heart, coffee exists on that continuum between the personal and the collective. In the same way individual prayer feeds and connects us to devotion amid a broader worshipping community, coffee can be enjoyed in isolation and with others. One method of consumption and enjoyment is not superior; rather, the varied experiences complement and amplify one another.

Just as no single, monolithic, correct way to do faith exists, there is no one right, proper method to drink coffee. The coffee journey blends trial, error, and discovery. I never trust people of faith who claim to have all the answers; nor do I trust coffee folks who proclaim their methods and opinions as gospel truth. Everyone has preferences, some deeply held and nurtured. When it comes to both coffee and faith, I certainly do.

Yet, without being open to new ideas, without remaining available to the possibilities of transformation, without allowing ourselves to be challenged by innovation, the joy of the journey is diminished. The coffee excursion parallels our ongoing search for inspiration and meaning, reminding us a fuller life exists beyond the visible world. Those unseen in our global economy are not truly invisible—it is our deficiency that we choose not to see them—and it is our charge to seek justice on their behalf.

The world's problems can seem overwhelming, and our power to exact change can feel ineffectual. Yet, the power to make a difference so often exists in the small acts performed in the spirit of community. Have a cup of coffee with a struggling friend and simply listen; make wise and informed choices when purchasing your coffee and know it makes a difference in the life of someone you will never meet; open your heart to the similarities of the human condition rather than dwelling on difference and isolation.

It's true that Jesus never sat around drinking coffee with his disciples, but he did share meals with those both inside and outside his regular circle. A key aspect of Jesus's ministry included eating and drinking with others and tearing down social boundaries and norms in the process. In an era of distrust among people of differing faiths and skin tones, sharing coffee with people of diverse backgrounds is a simple way to shatter the superficial walls that divide us.

Coffee can serve as the common ground to bridging difference and division. Perhaps that's the coffee bean's true potential, one that humanity has yet to fully unlock. Having coffee with a friend is energizing and pleasant; having coffee with a stranger draws us out of our comfort zones and forces us to leave our emotional silos. I encourage you to seek out ways to do both.

Sip deeply, friends, and enjoy the continuing pilgrimage of life, faith, and coffee.

ACKNOWLEDGMENTS

The General Confession from the 1662 Anglican *Book of Common Prayer* includes the line, "We acknowledge and bewail our manifold sins and wickedness." I don't intend to bewail much in this acknowledgments section—besides any sins of omission or misrepresentation for which I'm happy to accept responsibility—but I do want to acknowledge some folks without whom this book would not be possible.

First come the passionate, knowledgeable, and patient coffee professionals in my life who keep me caffeinated and abide my constant questions with grace and humor: Mike and Alicia Love of Coffee Labs Roasters in Tarrytown, New York, and Bob Weeks of Redeye Roasters in Hingham, Massachusetts. I literally couldn't have done this without you.

I'm grateful to the folks at Fortress Press for seeing the potential in this project, especially Beth Lewis (enjoy retirement!) and my editor and fellow coffee devotee Tony Jones. If you ever really want to get under his skin, put something in "scare quotes."

This book never would have come to fruition without the four-month sabbatical I took from my *real* job as rector of the Episcopal

Parish of St. John the Evangelist in Hingham, Massachusetts. I was consistently buoyed by the prayers and support of the entire congregation and the knowledge that things were in terrific and holy hands during my absence thanks to my able staff, gifted lay leaders, and especially the ministry of my assistant rector, the Reverend Noah Van Niel (even though he's exclusively a tea drinker).

My sabbatical travel was funded through a coveted Clergy Renewal Grant from the Lilly Endowment. This is an amazing program, and it allowed me to pursue these two passions—coffee and faith—in unique and life-giving ways.

There are a few people I'd like to thank from each specific stop on this journey. In Nicaragua, Francisco Javier Valle García and Bram de Hoog of Expocamo. Bram also proofed the sections involving coffee technicalities to ensure I got the complexities correct. In El Salvador, Gabriela Flores of J. Hill Beneficio. In Seattle, Tom Shaw and Ann-Marie Kurtz of Starbucks, and my friend since fourth grade Kevin Daniels. At St. Tikhon Monastery, Father Innocent and Brother Stephen. In Italy, our friends Harry, Andrea, and Madelaine Register, who met us in Rome to drink espresso and red wine. At Equal Exchange, the Interfaith Team—Susan Sklar, Peter Buck, and Bethany Karbowski.

I'm so thankful Hina Tai, journalist and associate director of research at *The Islamic Monthly*, enthusiastically responded to my out-of-the-blue request to read the portions of my manuscript relating to Islam. One of the joys of coffee is meeting people across faiths—both virtually and in real life.

I had a delightful and encouraging conversation with Rabbi Elliot Salo Schoenberg of The Rabbinical Assembly, an international organization of conservative rabbis in New York City. He's also a board member of Fair Trade Judaica, which is why I reached out to him.

My clergy comrades in coffee also need mention: the Reverend Scott Gunn, the Reverend Laurie Brock, and the Reverend David Sibley. Now stop sending me joke jars of Sanka!

The Reverend Rick Swanson and Tim Heath-Swanson, who keep us well caffeinated whenever we visit them in Vermont, remain valued members of our extended spiritual family.

The following local friends continue to keep me grounded and entertained, even if I always have to go to bed by 10:00 p.m. on Saturday nights to get up for the early Sunday morning service: Stephanie and Hans von der Luft, Tania and George Manning, and Peter and Nancy Wiley.

My brother Matt graciously read some early draft chapters to make sure the book would appeal to people beyond just the churchy crowd.

My mother-in-law, Rosalie Rogers, who continues to defy the stereotype about mothers-in-law, offered some helpful feedback on the manuscript. Sorry I couldn't work Proust in for you.

A few others who will get a kick out of seeing their names in print: Lexie and Teddy von der Luft; Gabby and Lexie Manning; Elsa, Linnea, and Liam Schenck. Hi Mom.

My boys, Benedict and Zachary, continue to inspire and delight me. I'm proud to be their dad, even when all they really want is for me to bring them an iced mocha latte home from Redeye Roasters.

Finally, to Bryna, thank you. For everything. Your passion for helping others at work and at home never ceases to amaze me. As a sign of my love, I think I'll go make you some coffee.

BIBLIOGRAPHY

Allen, Stewart Lee. *The Devil's Cup: Coffee, the Driving Force in History*. New York: Soho, 1999.

American Psychiatric Association. *Diagnostic and Statistical Manual of Mental Disorders*. 5th ed. Washington, DC: American Psychiatric Association, 2013.

Bakken, Gordon Morris, ed. *The World of the American West*. New York: Routledge, 2010.

Balin, Carole B. "'Good to the Last Drop': The Proliferation of the Maxwell House Haggadah." In *My People's Passover Haggadah: Traditional Texts, Modern Commentaries*, edited by Lawrence A. Hoffman and David Arnow, vol. 1, 85–90. Woodstock, VT: Jewish Lights Publishing, 2008.

Bartels, Lambert. *Oromo Religion: Myths and Rites of the Western Oromo of Ethiopia, an Attempt to Understand*. Berlin: D. Reimer, 1983.

Brown, Ruth. *Coffee Nerd: How to Have Your Coffee and Drink It Too*. Avon, MA: Adams Media, 2015.

Carrington, Damian. "Global Warming Brews Big Trouble for Coffee Birthplace Ethiopia." *The Guardian*, June 19, 2017. https://tinyurl.com/y9m6xg55.

Chrystal, Paul. *Coffee: A Drink for the Devil.* Stroud, UK: Amberley, 2016.

Cole, Adam. "Drink Coffee? Off with Your Head!" National Public Radio, January 17, 2012. https://tinyurl.com/y83ozc5d.

Crow, Jonathan. "J. S. Bach's Comic Opera, 'The Coffee Cantata,' Sings the Praises of the Great Stimulating Drink (1735)." Open Culture, June 12, 2014. https://tinyurl.com/y9mqchuv.

Davids, Kenneth. *Coffee: A Guide to Buying, Brewing, and Enjoying.* New York: Scribner, 1976.

DeCarlo, Jacqueline. *Fair Trade and How It Works.* New York: Rosen, 2011.

Eggers, Dave. *The Monk of Mokha.* New York: Knopf, 2018.

Fleming, Ian. *From Russia, with Love.* London: Jonathan Cape, 1957.

Freeman, James, Caitlin Freeman, and Tara Duggan. *The Blue Bottle Craft of Coffee.* Berkeley, CA: Ten Speed, 2012.

Haft, Michael, and Harrison Suarez. "The Marine's Secret Weapon: Coffee." *New York Times*, August 16, 2013. https://tinyurl.com/y76ygupu.

Hamblin, James. "A Brewing Problem," *The Atlantic*, March 2, 2013. https://tinyurl.com/y9vd8g99.

Hattox, Ralph S. *Coffee and Coffeehouses: The Origins of a Social Beverage in the Medieval Near East.* Seattle: University of Washington Press, 1985.

Hoffman, James. *The World Atlas of Coffee: From Beans to Brewing—Coffees Explored, Explained and Enjoyed.* London: Mitchell Beazley, 2014.

Horowitz, Elliott. "Coffee, Coffeehouses, and the Nocturnal Rites of Early Modern Jewry." *AJS Review* 14, no. 1 (Spring 1989): 17–46.

Jack, Albert. *What Caesar Did for My Salad: The Curious Stories Behind Our Favorite Foods*. New York: Perigee, 2014.

Jacob, Heinrich Eduard. *Coffee: The Epic of a Commodity*. Translated by Eden Paul and Cedar Paul. New York: Viking, 1935.

Koehler, Jeff. *Where the Wild Coffee Grows: The Untold Story of Coffee from the Cloud Forests of Ethiopia to Your Cup*. New York: Bloomsbury, 2017.

Läderach, Peter, Julian Ramirez-Villegas, Carlos Navarro-Racines, Carlos Zelaya, Armando Martinez-Valle, and Andy Jarvis. "Climate Change Adaptation of Coffee Production in Space and Time." *Climatic Change* 141, no. 1 (2017): 47. https://doi.org/10.1007/s10584-016-1788-9.

Lavine, Eileen M. "The Stimulating Story of Jews and Coffee." *Moment Magazine*, September 3, 2013. https://tinyurl.com/y87qmqxq.

Liberles, Robert. *Jews Welcome Coffee: Tradition and Innovation in Early Modern Germany*. Waltham, MA: Brandeis University Press, 2012.

Luttinger, Nina, and Gregory Dicum. *The Coffee Book: Anatomy of an Industry from Crop to the Last Drop*. New York: New Press, 2006.

Mehta, Ravi, Rui Zhu, and Amar Cheema. "Is Noise Always Bad? Exploring the Effects of Ambient Noise on Creative Cognition." *Journal of Consumer Research* 39, no. 4 (December 2012): 784–99.

The Men's Answer to the Women's Petition against Coffee: Vindicating Their Own Performances and the Virtues of that Liquor from the Undeserved Aspersions Lately Cast upon Them by Their Scandalous Pamphlet. London, 1674.

Multatuli. *Max Havelaar: Or, the Coffee Auctions of a Dutch Trading Company.* Translated by Roy Edwards. New York: Penguin, 1987.

Naironi, Antonius Faustus. *De Saluberrima Potione Cahue, Seu Café Nuncupata Discursus.* Rome: Michaelis Herculis, 1671.

O'Connell, Kim. "Soldiers Loved a Refreshing Cup of Coffee." *Civil War Times Magazine,* August 2014.

Olshan, Jeremy. "America's Coffee Cup Is Half Full." Market Watch, February 20, 2013. https://tinyurl.com/yclyug3x.

Parker, Scott F., and Michael W. Austin, eds. *Coffee: Philosophy for Everyone; Grounds for Debate.* Malden, MA: Wiley-Blackwell, 2011.

Pendergrast, Mark. *Uncommon Grounds: The History of Coffee and How It Transformed Our World.* New York: Basic, 2010.

Pinsker, Shachar M. *A Rich Brew: How Cafés Created Modern Jewish Culture.* New York: New York University Press, 2018.

Razavi, Lauren. "Movement to Pay It Forward with a Cup of Coffee Spills into US." National Public Radio, December 17, 2015. https://tinyurl.com/y8arf4f4.

Robinette, G. W. *The War on Coffee.* Valparaiso, Chile: Graffiti Militante Press, 2018.

Santlofer, Joy. *Food City: Four Centuries of Food-Making in New York.* New York: W. W. Norton, 2016.

Santos, Roseane M., and Darcy R. Lima. *An Unashamed Defense of Coffee: 101 Reasons to Drink Coffee without Guilt.* Bloomington, IN: Xlibris, 2009.

Schapira, Joel, David Schapira, and Karl Schapira. *The Book of Coffee and Tea.* New York: St. Martin's Press, 1975.

Schoenberg, Elliot Salo. "A Just Cup of Coffee." Fair Trade Judaica, December 9, 2013. https://tinyurl.com/y8rqhxx5.

Smith, Andrew F., ed. *The Oxford Encyclopedia of Food and Drink in America*. Oxford: Oxford University Press, 2013.

Soloway, Benjamin. "In Brazil's Coffee Industry, Some Workers Face 'Conditions Analogous to Slavery.'" *Foreign Policy*, April 13, 2016. https://tinyurl.com/y7uh7svr.

Stephenson, Tristan. *The Curious Barista's Guide to Coffee*. London: Ryland, Peters & Small, 2015.

Sterling, Justine. "A Brief, Delightful History of the Bundt Pan." *Food & Wine*, April 15, 2015. https://tinyurl.com/ycr69l62.

Stratton, Clifford J. "Caffeine—The Subtle Addiction." The Church of Jesus Christ of Latter-Day Saints, June 1988. https://tinyurl.com/yb9sc47c.

Ukers, William H. *All about Coffee*. New York: Tea and Coffee Trade Journal Company, 1922.

Van Arendonk, C. "Kahwa." In *Encyclopedia of Islam*. Leiden: Brill, 1978.

Wayessa, Bula Sirika. "Buna Qalaa: A Quest for Traditional Uses of Coffee among Oromo People with Special Emphasis on Wallaga, Ethiopia." *African Diaspora Archaeology Newsletter* 14, no. 3 (September 2011).

Weinberg, Bennett Alan, and Bonnie K. Bealer. *The World of Caffeine*. New York: Routledge, 2001.

Weissman, Jordan. "The Devious Ad Campaign That Convinced America Coffee Was Bad for Kids." *The Atlantic*, December 27, 2013. https://tinyurl.com/y9wazjn4.

Weissman, Michaele. *God in a Cup: The Obsessive Quest for the Perfect Coffee*. Hoboken, NJ: Wiley, 2008.

Wild, Antony. *Coffee: A Dark History*. New York: W. W. Norton, 2005.

Women's Petition against Coffee: Representing to Public Consideration the Grand Inconveniences Accruing to Their Sex from the Excessive Use of that Drying, Enfeebling, Liquor. London, 1674.

World Fair Trade Organization. *History of Fair Trade—60 Years of Fair Trade: A Brief History of the Fair Trade Movement*. Last updated 2015. https://tinyurl.com/ydz3m4k3.

Young, Christine Ellen. *A Bitter Brew: Faith, Power, and Poison in a Small New England Town*. New York: Berkley Books, 2005.

Zaimeche, Salah. "The Coffee Route from Yemen to London 10th–17th Centuries." Muslim Heritage, June 2003. https://tinyurl .com/y7x3x2pe.

NOTES

CHAPTER 2

1. Antonius Faustus Naironi, *De Saluberrima Potione Cahue, Seu Café Nuncupata Discursus* (Rome: Michaelis Herculis, 1671).
2. William H. Ukers, *All about Coffee* (New York: Tea and Coffee Trade Journal Company, 1922), 15.
3. Bennett Alan Weinberg and Bonnie K. Bealer, *The World of Caffeine* (New York: Routledge, 2001), 25.
4. Mark Pendergrast, *Uncommon Grounds: The History of Coffee and How It Transformed Our World* (New York: Basic, 2010), 4.
5. Kenneth Davids, *Coffee: A Guide to Buying, Brewing, and Enjoying* (New York: Scribner, 1976), 225.
6. Antony Wild, *Coffee: A Dark History* (New York: W. W. Norton, 2005), 50.
7. Ukers, *All about Coffee*, 17.
8. G. W. Robinette, *The War on Coffee* (Valparaiso, Chile: Graffiti Militante Press, 2018), 249.
9. Adam Cole, "Drink Coffee? Off with Your Head!," National Public Radio, January 17, 2012, https://tinyurl.com/y83ozc5d.
10. Sheikh Ansari Djezeri Hanball Abd-al-Kadir, 1587, quoted in Heinrich Eduard Jacob, *Coffee: The Epic of a Commodity*, trans. Eden Paul and Cedar Paul (New York: Viking, 1935), 18.

CHAPTER 4

1. C. Van Arendonk, "Kahwa," in *Encyclopedia of Islam* (Leiden: Brill, 1978), 450.
2. Bennett Alan Weinberg and Bonnie K. Bealer, *The World of Caffeine* (New York: Routledge, 2001), 11.
3. Van Arendonk, "Kahwa," 450.
4. Ralph S. Hattox, *Coffee and Coffeehouses: The Origins of a Social Beverage in the Medieval Near East* (Seattle: University of Washington Press, 1985), 28.
5. Elliott Horowitz, "Coffee, Coffeehouses, and the Nocturnal Rites of Early Modern Jewry," *AJS Review* 14, no. 1 (Spring 1989): 17–46.

CHAPTER 5

1. William Ukers, *All about Coffee* (New York: Tea and Coffee Trade Journal Company, 1922), 26.
2. Albert Jack, *What Caesar Did for My Salad: The Curious Stories Behind Our Favorite Foods* (New York: Perigee, 2014), 3.
3. Jonathoa Crow, "J. S. Bach's Comic Opera, 'The Coffee Cantata,' Sings the Praises of the Great Stimulating Drink (1735)," Open Culture, June 12, 2014, https://tinyurl.com/y9mqchuv.
4. Ukers, *All about Coffee*, 46.
5. Tristan Stephenson, *The Curious Barista's Guide to Coffee* (London: Ryland, Peters & Small, 2015), 87–88.

CHAPTER 6

1. Eileen M. Lavine, "The Stimulating Story of Jews and Coffee," *Moment Magazine*, September 3, 2013, https://tinyurl.com/y87qmqxq.
2. Robert Liberles, *Jews Welcome Coffee: Tradition and Innovation in Early Modern Germany* (Waltham, MA: Brandeis University Press, 2012), 62.
3. Elliot Salo Schoenberg, "A Just Cup of Coffee," Fair Trade Judaica, December 9, 2013, https://tinyurl.com/y8rqhxx5.
4. Antony Wood, *Athenae Oxonienses, 1691*, quoted in Ralph Hattox, *Coffee and Coffeehouses: The Origins of a Social Beverage in the Medieval Near East* (Seattle: University of Washington Press, 1985), 13.

5. Shachar M. Pinsker, introduction to *A Rich Brew: How Cafés Created Modern Jewish Culture* (New York: New York University Press, 2018).

6. Carole B. Balin, "'Good to the Last Drop': The Proliferation of the Maxwell House Haggadah," in *My People's Passover Haggadah: Traditional Texts, Modern Commentaries*, ed. Lawrence A. Hoffman and David Arnow, vol. 1 (Woodstock, VT: Jewish Lights Publishing, 2008), 85–90.

7. Roseane M. Santos and Darcy R. Lima, *An Unashamed Defense of Coffee: 101 Reasons to Drink Coffee without Guilt* (Bloomington, IN: Xlibris, 2009), 129.

8. Justine Sterling, "A Brief, Delightful History of the Bundt Pan," *Food & Wine*, April 15, 2015, https://tinyurl.com/ycr69l62.

9. Antony Wild, *Coffee: A Dark History* (New York: W. W. Norton, 2005), 18.

CHAPTER 7

1. Lambert Bartels, *Oromo Religion: Myths and Rites of the Western Oromo of Ethiopia, an Attempt to Understand* (Berlin: D. Reimer, 1983).

2. Bula Sirika Wayessa, "Buna Qalaa: A Quest for Traditional Uses of Coffee among Oromo People with Special Emphasis on Wallaga, Ethiopia," *African Diaspora Archaeology Newsletter* 14, no. 3 (September 2011).

3. Ruth Brown, *Coffee Nerd: How to Have Your Coffee and Drink It Too* (Avon, MA: Adams Media, 2015), 33.

4. Ian Fleming, *From Russia, with Love* (London: Jonathan Cape, 1957), chapter 11.

5. Jeff Koehler, *Where the Wild Coffee Grows: The Untold Story of Coffee from the Cloud Forests of Ethiopia to Your Cup* (New York: Bloomsbury, 2017), 217.

CHAPTER 8

1. Bennett Alan Weinberg and Bonnie K. Bealer, *The World of Caffeine* (New York: Routledge, 2001), 181.

2. Nina Luttinger and Gregory Dicum, *The Coffee Book: Anatomy of an Industry from Crop to the Last Drop* (New York: New Press, 2006), 31.

3. Joel Schapira, David Schapira, and Karl Schapira, *The Book of Coffee and Tea* (New York: St. Martin's Press, 1975), 20.
4. Schapira, Schapira, and Schapira, *Book of Coffee and Tea*, 21.
5. Andrew F. Smith, ed., *The Oxford Encyclopedia of Food and Drink in America* (Oxford: Oxford University Press, 2013), 266.
6. Scott F. Parker and Michael W. Austin, eds., *Coffee: Philosophy for Everyone; Grounds for Debate* (Malden, MA: Wiley-Blackwell, 2011), chapter 7.
7. Kim O'Connell, "Soldiers Loved a Refreshing Cup of Coffee," *Civil War Times Magazine*, August 2014.
8. Gordon Morris Bakken, ed., *The World of the American West* (New York: Routledge, 2010), 354.
9. Michael Haft and Harrison Suarez, "The Marine's Secret Weapon: Coffee," *New York Times*, August 16, 2013, https://tinyurl.com/y76ygupu.
10. Joy Santlofer, *Food City: Four Centuries of Food-Making in New York* (New York: W. W. Norton, 2016), 264.
11. Jeremy Olshan, "America's Coffee Cup Is Half Full," Market Watch, February 20, 2013, https://tinyurl.com/yclyug3x.
12. Mark Pendergrast, *Uncommon Grounds: The History of Coffee and How It Transformed Our World* (New York: Basic, 2010), 156.

CHAPTER 10

1. Salah Zaimeche, "The Coffee Route from Yemen to London 10th–17th Centuries," Muslim Heritage, June 2003, https://tinyurl.com/y7x3x2pe.
2. Antony Wild, *Coffee: A Dark History* (New York: W. W. Norton, 2005), 53.
3. Wild, *Coffee*, 88.
4. Mark Pendergrast, *Uncommon Grounds: The History of Coffee and How It Transformed Our World* (New York: Basic, 2010), 12.
5. *The Women's Petition against Coffee: Representing to Public Consideration the Grand Inconveniences Accruing to Their Sex from the Excessive Use of that Drying, Enfeebling, Liquor* (London, 1674).
6. *The Men's Answer to the Women's Petition against Coffee: Vindicating Their Own Performances and the Virtues of that Liquor from the Undeserved*

Aspersions Lately Cast upon Them by Their Scandalous Pamphlet (London, 1674).

7. Ravi Mehta, Rui Zhu, and Amar Cheema, "Is Noise Always Bad? Exploring the Effects of Ambient Noise on Creative Cognition," *Journal of Consumer Research* 39, no. 4 (December 2012): 784–99.

8. Lauren Razavi, "Movement to Pay It Forward with a Cup of Coffee Spills into US," National Public Radio, December 17, 2015, https://tinyurl.com/y8arf4f4.

CHAPTER 11

1. Antony Wild, *Coffee: A Dark History* (London: W. W. Norton, 2005), 98.

2. Nina Luttinger and Gregory Dicum, *The Coffee Book: Anatomy of an Industry from Crop to the Last Drop* (New York: New Press, 2006), 27.

3. Mark Pendergrast, *Uncommon Grounds: The History of Coffee and How It Transformed Our World* (New York: Basic, 2010), 17.

4. Pendergrast, *Uncommon Grounds*, 23.

5. Wild, *Coffee*, 230.

6. Benjamin Soloway, "In Brazil's Coffee Industry, Some Workers Face 'Conditions Analogous to Slavery,'" *Foreign Policy*, April 13, 2016, https://tinyurl.com/y7uh7svr.

7. Jeff Woodworth, "The Word of Wisdom," The Church of Jesus Christ of Latter Day Saints, Church History, June 11, 2013, https://tinyurl.com/y8lup8zt.

8. Clifford J. Stratton, "Caffeine—The Subtle Addiction," The Church of Jesus Christ of Latter-Day Saints, June 1988, https://tinyurl.com/yb9sc47c.

9. Jordan Weissman, "The Devious Ad Campaign That Convinced America Coffee Was Bad for Kids," *The Atlantic*, December 27, 2013, https://tinyurl.com/y9wazjn4.

10. American Psychiatric Association, *Diagnostic and Statistical Manual of Mental Disorders*, 5th ed. (Washington, DC: American Psychiatric Association, 2013).

CHAPTER 12

1. Jacqueline DeCarlo, *Fair Trade and How It Works* (New York: Rosen, 2011), 57.

2. *History of Fair Trade—60 Years of Fair Trade: A Brief History of the Fair Trade Movement*, World Fair Trade Organization, last updated 2015, https://tinyurl.com/ydz3m4k3.

3. Multatuli, *Max Havelaar: Or, the Coffee Auctions of a Dutch Trading Company*, trans. Roy Edwards (New York: Penguin, 1987).

4. Milton Friedman, "The Social Responsibility of Business Is to Increase Its Profits," *New York Times Magazine*, 1970.

CHAPTER 13

1. Damian Carrington, "Global Warming Brews Big Trouble for Coffee Birthplace Ethiopia," *The Guardian*, June 19, 2017, https://tinyurl.com/y9m6xg55.

2. Peter Läderach, Julian Ramirez-Villegas, Carlos Navarro-Racines, Carlos Zelaya, Armando Martinez-Valle, and Andy Jarvis, "Climate Change Adaptation of Coffee Production in Space and Time," *Climatic Change* 141, no. 1 (2017): 47, https://doi.org/10.1007/s10584-016-1788-9.

3. James Hamblin, "A Brewing Problem," *The Atlantic*, March 2, 2013, https://tinyurl.com/y9vd8g99.

CHAPTER 14

1. Christine Ellen Young, *A Bitter Brew: Faith, Power, and Poison in a Small New England Town* (New York: Berkley Books, 2005).

2. Associated Press, "Poisoner's Suicide Note Says He Acted Alone," April 22, 2006.

Schenck, Tim

6662-14
9/19

DATE DUE